Room
recipes

COOKING UP STYLE WITH COLOR

See the Yellow Pages under *Paint-Retail* for the Benjamin Moore
retailer closest to you.

Benjamin Moore PAINTS

A STROKE OF BRILLIANCE®

TORONTO • MONTREAL • VANCOUVER

NEWARK • BOSTON • RICHMOND • JACKSONVILLE • JOHNSTON • CLEVELAND • CHICAGO

ST. LOUIS • HOUSTON • BIRMINGHAM • DENVER • LOS ANGELES • SANTA CLARA

First published in 2000 by
Benjamin Moore & Co., Limited
139 Mulock Avenue
Toronto, Ontario
M6N 2G9

9393 boul. St-Michel
Montreal, Quebec
H1Z 3H3

26680 Gloucester Way
Aldergrove, British Columbia
V4W 3V6

ISBN 0-9686088-0-9

Produced by
Publications-Plus Inc.
2330 Millrace Court, Unit 2
Mississauga, Ontario
L5N 1W2

Printed and bound in Canada
Second Printing, Revised Edition

....

Editor: Diane McDougall-Tierney
Book design: Derek Chung
Cover concept: Michael Cross
Photography: Ted Yarwood
House project liaison: Peggy Sheffield
Copy editor: Linda Stulberg
Film and print: Colour Innovations
Paint deposits: McCorquodale Color Card,
                               Div. of Rexam Canada Limited

Jane Lockhart's

Room
recipes

COOKING UP STYLE WITH COLOR

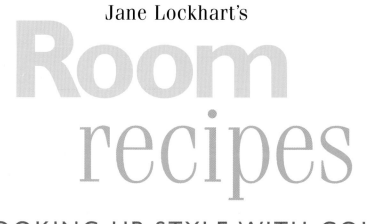

DECORATIVE PAINT EFFECTS
SPICY DESIGN DETAILS
WINDOW DRESSINGS
IDEAS FOR EVERY TASTE
ROOM RECIPE CARDS INSIDE

Con**tents**

PAGE 51   PAGE 55   PAGE 61   PAGE 67   PAGE 73

Contri**butors**

There are many people who deserve a hearty thanks for their work in producing this book. Paramount to the production was the assistance of Mattamy Homes and their generous loan of one of their premier homes. Our design team is a unique blend of talents and personalities. These contributors have been integral to this project:

THE DESIGN TEAM

BRAD JENSEN

Brad Jensen, faux-finish artist and painter, started his own company, Jensen Interiors, in 1989. In addition to private commissions, ranging from light construction to faux finishes, Jensen also contributed to Benjamin Moore's *Paint a Great Impression*. His work has appeared on *One House, Two Looks* and *This Small Space* on HGTV and Citytv's *CityLine*. His work has also been featured in *Canadian Living* and *Style at Home* magazines.

SHARON GRECH

A senior color and design associate at Benjamin Moore & Co., Limited in Toronto, Sharon Grech applies her professional design skills to the development and merchandising of the company's products in Canada and takes a leading role in national and regional marketing. Her responsibilities include monitoring color trends, and demonstrating the company's products at home shows, trade shows and in print and broadcast media. As a faux-finish artist, she is a regular guest on Citytv's *CityLine* as well as at seminars and workshops.

Grech contributed to Benjamin Moore's top-selling book *Paint A Great Impression*. She is a graduate of the art and art history programs at the University of Toronto.

MARY DOBSON

When Mary Dobson, a freelance design consultant and writer, wants to change the look of a home, she doesn't reach for a toolbox, she reaches for her sewing machine. As a creator of fabric design projects, she is a sought-after guest for TV shows such as Citytv's *CityLine*, as well as home shows, craft seminars and workshops in Canada and the U.S.

She is the co-author of *Do-It-Yourself Projects from A to Z*, published by Lansing Buildall, which features home improvements using paint and fabric. She is also a regular presenter for Benjamin Moore's "Interior Imagination" seminar.

Dobson has contributed design projects for national magazines, such as *Canadian Living* and *Style at Home*. Her projects appeal to a wide range of audiences, from young families watching their budget to empty-nesters looking for timeless elegance.

Dobson is a graduate in home economics from Mount Saint Vincent University in Halifax.

JASON SQUIRES

Jason Squires has been working in television for the past five years in jobs ranging from camera operator to props and production coordinator. He has worked on shows including HGTV's *One House, Two Looks* and *Craftscapes* on the Life Network. For this book, Squires acted as production coordinator, site manager and liaison with our contributing companies.

SPECIAL CONTRIBUTORS ON-SITE

JACINTA COOPER

Jacinta Cooper started her own interior-design consulting company, Kairos Creative Design Studio, in Toronto in 1997. Her projects range from residential, retail and corporate clients, to hospitality and architectural design firms. She has also worked on TV shows, such as *Design for Living* on HGTV Canada.

Cooper, who was born in England, studied fine arts at the University of Calgary and completed her interior-design degree at the University of Manitoba in Winnipeg.

SNEZANA BACANIN

Snezana Bacanin has had a strong appreciation for art since the age of 7, when she visited an art gallery showcasing the work of The Group of Seven. Today, Bacanin is a secondary-school teacher who continues to delight others with her creative talents through her own home decor projects and contagious enthusiasm.

ADDITIONAL ASSISTANCE

Sandro and Peter Di Poce of S&P Painting, completed all the exterior painting – three times, no less! Ken Balcer built the deck as well as some small, but complicated carpentry projects inside the house. Essential help was provided by several other individuals. Charlene Ericsson, stylist, was in charge of propping for the house. Landscape design and plantings were provided by John Reeves. Student painters were on hand from the Craftsman Painter Program. Louanne Rudisuela from Benjamin Moore was critically important in answering questions, as well as keeping us on track. Sarah Maslin, Scarlett Ballantyne and Francine Alepins, all Benjamin Moore designers, lent creative hands to the project.

See *Sources*, page 87, for furniture and accessories contributors.

Fore**word**

Color has become a hot topic in North America — and not just in home decor. And yet, its significance in decorating is rarely singled out as a major contributor to the atmosphere of a room.

Not surprisingly, there are books available on every possible approach to color — from color psychology to those solely devoted to colorful photographs of room settings.

So, what could possibly be new about this color book?

For starters, we began with an incredible series of new colors from Benjamin Moore Paints called the *Regal Signature Color Collection*. Then, we integrated these 99 deep vibrant colors with Benjamin Moore's 2,000 existing colors — they are showcased throughout this book.

Our actual "home base" is a real house in which we've incorporated 11 completely unique and individual decorating styles, one per room. In addition, we've explored the use of different color palettes and projects for the exterior. With this nontypical approach to a home decor book, we illustrate the valuable role color plays — not just in creating a room setting, but in establishing the *style* of that space.

Borrowing from another popular interest — food preparation and cooking — we approach color as one of the main ingredients in the creation of the overall environment of a "roomscape." The form of this book then, is that of a cookbook — each of the 11 styles or "dishes" served follows the format of a recipe — a "Room Recipe." Of course, a dash of creativity is a welcome addition to any recipe, as it provides a more personal flavor.

Another exciting aspect of this book is its entirely new printing process. The colors of each "color menu" have actually been deposited on the page. These are real color samples. This process eliminates the common problem of color shifts when photographs are printed.

We hope you enjoy our collection of "Room Recipes" and that our style and color choices engage and inspire you to jump into a world of new colors.

JANE LOCKHART

CHAPTER ONE

Cooking up **color**

HOW YOU VIEW COLOR

The structure of the eye influences how colors appear. For instance, warm colors, such as reds, tend to advance in our sight, because red light rays focus on the back of our eye. This makes the color appear to move forward. Cool colors, such as blue, are focused on the front of the eye, giving the illusion of a receding color. Greens are focused by the center of the eye and are therefore easier to interpret. If you have ever wondered why green is considered the color of concentration, this is why. The eye and hence the brain don't have to work too hard to interpret the color, so more energy can go into the task at hand, rather than the color on the wall. Darker colors seem heavier than lighter tints, because deep colors absorb more light, instead of reflecting the color back to our eyes.

So, color choices have a lot more to do with the value and contrast of the color rather than the color itself. Be sure to study all characteristics of a color in relation to other colors, not as an isolated color.

YOUR BEST MIXING TOOL

Color is actually light, so, it's not surprising that the first color wheel was created after Sir Isaac Newton's discovery of white light and its color spectrum. Getting to know and understand the color wheel will greatly help you choose colors, even in this modern day and age.

Scientist Moses Harris created the first color wheel in 1770 to classify red, yellow and blue as primary colors. These three colors are the basis of all others, because they can't be created by mixing any other colors together. This classification of primary colors was accepted by most artists in the 19th century.

In the early 20th century, as modern art took hold, Johannes Itten, a German teacher, art theorist and painter, enlarged the basic color wheel to include secondary and tertiary colors. Itten's color wheel is the one with which we are most familiar today.

Despite Itten's best efforts to simplify the complex relationships of colors, most people do not use the color wheel to decorate their homes because they still see it as something for artists only. This is unfortunate, because it is a practical and easy way to put a pleasant color scheme together. Here's how it can work for you.

This rainbow of colors is known as the visual spectrum. It ranges from red to violet and is the purest form of each color family. These colors are often referred to as primary colors. The first three colors are warm colors, because they contain some yellow, while the other three are cool colors, because they have blue in them. Complements are red and green, orange and blue or yellow and purple.

WARM
COOL
WARM
COOL
The color wheel

Basic ingredients

COMPLEMENTARY COLORS

To create a personal scheme for your home with unique appeal, select a combination of complementary colors. Complementary colors are those that are opposite to each other on the color wheel. When two opposite colors are placed together, they complement each other and are pleasing to the eye.

Generally, when most of us think of complements, we think of the bright, bold color combinations, instead of today's more current complementary color schemes, such as burgundy combined with sage green

(red/green), light peach combined with gray-blue (orange/blue) or lavender and butter yellow (purple/yellow). If you have difficulty selecting a scheme, use the color wheel and choose a complementary pairing.

ANALOGOUS COLORS

Analogous colors are those that are beside each other on the color wheel. Using colors that blend with one another creates a more restful, less intense, color palette. Select analogous colors and use them together to create a room with less contrast. For example, yellow and green blend to make a room that is softer in appearance, but still strong in its design.

WARM AND COOL TEMPERATURES

Ittens also developed the concept of warm versus cool colors. He based this on the notion that some colors have a blue undertone, while others have a yellow one. It is these tones that determine the "temperature" of a color.

How is this useful to you? When you can distinguish which colors are cool and which are warm, it is easier to choose the right colors for the atmosphere you want to create. Remember, though, that any color can have a warm or cool base. For example, if you choose blue for your living room but you don't want it to feel too cold or bleak, select one that has a yellow, rather than a green, undertone to it.

Serving up **style**

COLOR AND SPACE

To choose the right color for your room, you need to decide what the space will be used for – and the style you want. Will the space be used for entertaining? Should it be lively? Or is it a room for peace and quiet? If so, your colors should be cool and calming. Function will determine the fixtures and furnishings needed – whether your decor style is modern, traditional or country.

Once your style choice has been made, then color choices become easier. Contrary to popular belief, dark colors do not make a room look smaller, any more than light colors make a room look larger. After all, if a room is 8 feet by 10 feet, it will always be that size, regardless of the color choice!

What becomes important is how color choices are combined to emphasize and feature the best aspects of a room. Contrast of color is what influences the visual size.

COLOR CONTRAST

Color contrast is the comparison of one color to another within a space. Dark colors do not make a room look smaller; rather, it is contrast that makes a room appear smaller. The light in a room appears less when a dark color is on the wall because the dark color absorbs more light.

The more contrast there is, and the more variations of contrast there are within a

Complementary colors come in tints as well. Tints are the pastel colors that many of us remember from the 1980s. White has been added to each color to create a lighter color than the original. Combine these colors with each other for a soft effect in a room – or add them to a brighter color scheme for some light punch.

This rich collection of colors is also the visual spectrum, but here black has been added to each of the colors. These colors are known as shades. Complements still exist when colors are darkened, but are less intense than when viewed side by side. The depth of these colors makes them lush and full.

LIGHT: KEEPING IT WARM OR COOL

There are two types of light commonly used throughout homes. Generally, kitchens have fluorescent lights, and living spaces have incandescent. These types of lights are drastically different from each other, as one is a cool light and the other is warm light. A color in one room may look drastically different in another room based solely on the type of lighting. When choosing a paint color in the paint store, be sure to take it home to view under the lighting conditions within that space, to really see what it will look like.

Incandescent lighting

This type of light has a warm yellow glow to it. It is soft on facial features and enhances yellow tones. Blues will look grayer in this type of light.

Fluorescent lighting

This type of light, often considered harsher on skin tones than incandescent, is generally blue-based or cool in color. It will enhance cool tones, such as cool blues and greens. However, there are warm-toned fluorescent lamps that more closely mimic incandescent.

The best type of fluorescent lamp to use in your home is a full-spectrum bulb. It is cleaner and brighter than normal fluorescent tubes, and its light is white, so that colors are more accurate.

→

space, the smaller a room appears. This is because the contrast of a dark wall color, adjacent to a light one, helps to define the architecture and therefore the size of the space more clearly.

In addition, adding contrasting furniture in a variety of colors will visually decrease the size of the space. This is because your eye jumps around the room, trying to absorb all the objects in view. This results in what appears to be a smaller space, but not necessarily an uninteresting space.

If you use one color throughout, combined with tints and shades of that color, you create a monochromatic scheme. Regardless of whether it is a dark color or a light one, the room will feel larger. However, how the room looks and expresses your personal style is more important than the visual size of the room.

MIXING WITH CONTRAST

Using contrasting colors is almost more important than the actual tone of a color for a room, because it deals with the relationship of one color to another.

Contrast can be used to enhance objects that are both uniquely personal and interesting. We often focus too much on the specific color choice for walls, ceilings and floors, instead of how the colors blend and balance to best showcase our personal items. Your furniture, fixtures and accessories are an extension of your personal taste. The colors on your walls and floors should be chosen to enhance these elements, not compete with them.

To tame an old brown sofa's influence on your decor style, use contrast to lower its visual emphasis. Rather than placing it against a stark white wall, which would result in high contrast, place it against a beige, brown or taupe wall, so that it doesn't stand out as much. Even if brown is a color you dislike, it is better to add more of it to help integrate the existing brown piece. Having only one item in a certain color actually makes it stand out, rather than blend in. Balance is achieved by reducing high levels of contrast.

To sharpen the look of a faded white chair, place it against a darker background. In relative contrast, the chair looks brighter and stands out more against a surface that does not compete with it, but rather complements it.

SPICING UP ARCHITECTURAL FEATURES

Perhaps one of the most important areas to apply the concepts of contrast is on existing architectural features of your home. Radiators or wall vents, for example, should be selected in colors that have little to no contrast with the surfaces around them. This is a method of hiding these objects, so that they do not become unsightly features in the room.

CEILINGS

One of the most overlooked surfaces in any room is the ceiling. All too often, it is simply painted white by default. Visually, we are attracted to brighter objects before darker objects. White has the highest reflective value of all colors, which means we are more inclined to see it.

As a result, bright white ceilings actually draw attention away from the objects we want guests to view. We forget that there are "six sides" to a room, not five.

The ceiling should also be an important consideration in the color choices for the room. Adding a dash of the wall color to the

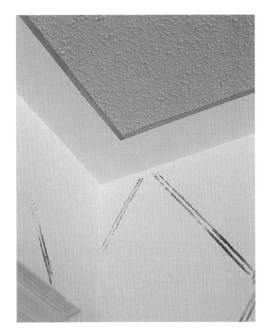

ceiling paint can help lower the stark contrast of the ceiling and make it part of the design.

ARCHITECTURAL TREATS: CROWN MOLDING AND TRIM

Crown molding is a feature that enhances the appearance of a room. Few people, however, give this wonderful feature the attention it deserves. Based on the idea of contrast, crown molding should be visually identifiable. Yet it is often painted white, the same color as the ceiling. As a result, this wonderful feature is not as strong as it could be. Should you choose to leave the crown molding white, a touch of any tint of color to the ceiling paint is the best way to emphasize it. Not only does this minimize the visual brightness of the ceiling, it also helps to make the crown molding an important architectural element.

Trim and baseboards can be strong features if they are more than three inches in height. Strengthen their appearance by contrasting their color with the surfaces against which they are placed. If your trim is not a feature you want to highlight, paint it the same color as the wall to make it disappear altogether. Or paint it a few shades deeper than the wall color, so that it recedes.

Delightful **texture**

FROM SMOOTH TO CRUNCHY

As tone-on-tone and monochromatic color schemes gain popularity, texture and sheen in furnishings, materials and fixtures become more important to provide interest.

Since texture is often a subtle element of a material, it is easier to add unique textures within a space without compromising the overall unity of the room. Combining contrasting textures that are quite different, such as rough/smooth, light/dark or hard/soft, can create interest. Each texture picks up light and shadows within the space differently to provide subtle color changes.

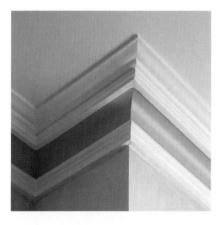

HOW TEXTURE AFFECTS COLOR

As texture changes, it alters the appearance of a color. For example, deeply textured surfaces, such as a honeycomb pattern, create many more dark and light colors than a simple pin-dot pattern.

Sheen affects the look of texture and changes the appearance of colors within a space. Flat surfaces with

Although computers have been designed to assist us in numerous daily tasks, the one area where they aren't helpful is in selecting colors for your home. There are color-matching computer systems that do help with initial planning ideas. However, it is unwise to use a computer when determining actual color choices, because a computer sample is different from an actual color chip.

A color sample produced by a computer will also look quite different from that on the screen. Why? Although the colors may be designed to look the same, there is a difference in how they are produced. Computer and television color is made from pixels of light, which come together to form the images that we read as pictures from a distance. A paint chip, fabric swatch or textile is colored with pigments.

This is called *additive* and *subtractive* color. Additive color is the method of adding colors together to create a new one. This also applies to lighting where one color layered on another creates yet another one.

Subtractive color occurs when one color added to another cancels out the first one. This is how the pigments of paints, dyes and inks work. The easiest way to remember this is that when you mix all colors of light together, you create white, but when you mix all pigment colors together, you create black.

little or no gloss absorb light. They appear lighter than those with gloss, which reflect light. In fact, the more sheen you add to a paint color, the darker the color appears because it reflects more light.

Monochromatic schemes can be enhanced by the combination of shiny and matte surfaces throughout.

SAVORY NEUTRALS

Most people believe that neutral colors are beige or gray. In fact, neutrals can be any colors that dominate a space. In nature, for instance, a blue sky and green grass are neutrals. Set against these neutral colors are all the other colors of life – flowers, birds, stones and more.

In a home environment, the best way to camouflage a fixed item you don't like is to add more of that color. If, for instance, you have mustard-colored bathroom fixtures, do not try to decorate as if they didn't exist. Although you may be able to overlook them, the reality is that your guests will see them. By working with the color – adding yellow to the walls, for example, you will make them less powerful visually.

"The color of the front of the door should match that of the room it faces. It is only the back of the door that takes on the color of the room that it closes off."

CHAPTER TWO

Working up an appetite

RELISH THE FUN

When choosing a color scheme, take a moment to simply relish the fun of decorating. Select anything whose colors you like – from a child's brightly colored marble to a hand-painted bowl you bought as a souvenir. Absorb the colors and remember them when the time comes for selecting a color scheme.

Feel free to experiment – at least at the inspirational stage of your project. Have fun and don't let fear curb what could be a really creative and unique solution. When you have selected a color palette that both inspires and excites you, you'll have a sound base on which to build your home decor.

Never underestimate the power of the *wow* factor. Color is the fastest way to add pizzazz to any room, no matter how dismal it may seem. Strive for impact. After all, a space that has *wow* is a space that has true character and pleases the senses.

COOKING UP IDEAS

Although the task of decorating your home is enormous, it is best to divide the project into stages, so that the job does not seem so overwhelming.

Start at your front door. If you live in a house, look at it from the outside to understand its style and character. See if there is a feature on the outside that you wish to carry throughout the inside of your home. For example, if your home has a Victorian-style porch and trimmings, consider carrying this theme inside with the color palette of that era.

Conversely, feel free to rebel against the outside shell of your home. If you live in a modern high-rise condo but dream of living in the Caribbean, you may want to create an entirely different feel on the inside. Choose the bright neon colors of the islands, if that's your dream decor.

The easiest way to begin any design project – whether it is a room or an entire house – is to create a materials sample board. Collect samples of all the materials you wish to use throughout the space and glue them onto sturdy cardboard or wood. Include all major surfaces, e.g., flooring, walls and counters. And don't forget your inspiration: be sure to add pictures of the items that inspired your look in order to create the overall feel of the space.

ARE YOU FINISHED?

After some consideration, most of us can determine where a color should start and stop in a home. But here is some guidance for those areas where it may not be so clear.

Color should follow what you see when you walk through your home. This means that if you see the corner of the hallway wall before the living room, then the color of the hallway should flow into the living room from the hall – not the other way around.

This prevents viewing a bit of color before seeing it in the full context of the room. Other examples of this include:

1. The opening of a room that doesn't have a casing or door trim In this instance, the wall of the opening should be painted the same color as the walls of the first room that is viewed.

2. Changing colors between floors When color of the main-floor hallway flows downstairs to the basement or upstairs to the bedrooms, change colors for this new area at a corner. Select the corner that is out of view from the upper hall, so that the upstairs color is not compromised.

3. The backs of doors The color of the front of the door should match that of the room it faces. This color should also wrap around the edges of the door. The back of the door should take on the color of the room it closes off.

Starting from **scratch**

WHAT FLOOR PLAN DO YOU HAVE?

Begin by identifying your floor plan. This will dictate your color and style choices. There are two common plans. The first is a traditional floor plan, where each room is a separate space closed off by a door or doorway.

An open-concept floor plan is one in which each room either visually or physically flows into the next. There are few walls, and the space feels more like one large space. Although natural light fills these homes and the flow is comfortable and easy, they are more difficult to decorate because the look of each room influences the next.

When selecting flooring for either of these plans, try to unify as many rooms as possible by choosing consistent flooring throughout. If you change flooring materials and still want to create good visual flow, then choose a different floor material but in a similar color. The contrast from one surface to the next will not be so stark. If you wish to use different colors in each room, create unity by using the same color on the trim and baseboards.

DECORATING A TRADITIONAL-STYLE PLAN

In a traditional-style home, each room is separated from the next. The challenge is tying them together. The easiest way to do this is to find a common color or style of furniture to be used throughout each space.

For example, if the dining room walls are painted an eggplant color, then the living room could feature eggplant-color cushions on the sofa. This creates continuity between the main rooms. As long as there is some link between the rooms and their colors, then there will be consistency throughout.

Adjacent rooms do not have to be identical. However, to create some flow of style, add at least one common element throughout, whether it is a color, pattern, texture or motif. This can be done simply by carrying a color throughout, using throw pillows in one room and picture frames in the next.

DECORATING AN OPEN-CONCEPT PLAN

The challenge with this floor plan is how to add a variety of colors to the space – and knowing when to stop or start each color.

In this type of home, a common theme in color and style is essential. It is especially important in open-concept floor plans, because so much is visible.

Select a palette of colors that matches the furnishings, but choose no more than five colors. Although this may sound limited, remember that each color has an infinite number of tints and shades that can be used in combination with all the other palette choices. A color can stop in any corner and a new color can begin, but there should be a visible element that ties them all together. Highlight architectural features, such as fireplaces, alcoves or accent walls, with the same colors, so that they add punch to the decor. Or use the same tones of color throughout, in different tints and shades.

PUBLIC VERSUS PRIVATE SPACE

When you examine your home plan, whether it is traditional or open-concept, notice the actual layout and positioning of rooms. This will give you clues as to what colors will be flowing into the next. In addition, determine how you will move through your living space. If you intend to use the main-floor front room as a private office, rather than a TV or family room, then your color choices – and therefore the color flow – within the space will change.

Generally there are two types of space within your home: public and private space. Public space is the space that friends, family and visitors see when they come to your home. These rooms usually include the powder room, hallway, entry, living and dining rooms, and occasionally the family room and kitchen, depending on the style of your home.

Private space is the area that family and only selected guests see on a daily basis. This includes the family bathroom and ensuite, bedrooms and possibly the office or den.

COLORS FOR PUBLIC SPACE

To make your public spaces flow from one area to the next in a pleasing manner, visually link them by choosing colors that are part of one scheme.

To begin, select an important piece of fabric from furniture or window coverings that you intend to keep. Choose something you want to make a focal point or connecting element of the rooms. Make sure that this piece has a variety of colors in it, so you have some color choices from which to work.

From this item, choose three to five colors to create a main palette. These will be the main colors that are repeated throughout the public areas. Remember that you can always use tints and shades of these colors as well.

Select a variety of different colors for walls of individual rooms, or choose one color throughout but accent it with the other four colors in each area. To unify your color choice in the public areas, be sure that the original textile or material that created the palette is visible.

COLORS FOR PRIVATE SPACE

These individual rooms have separate functions, so the design and style can be completely different for each. Don't worry if the bedrooms do not match the living and dining rooms. These are spaces that do not run together, nor will these rooms be seen by most guests.

Private space is not part of the overall house flow unless you want it to be. In fact, it is a pleasant break to have the main parts of the house one color and style, while the bedrooms are another. You can also be more daring in private rooms. After all, a bedroom is a private room and should be treated as a getaway – something different than the rest of the house and day-to-day living.

STICKY SITUATIONS

Difficult rooms are those with fixed items that are expensive or time-consuming to remove. One example is a bathroom with dated fixtures in brown, harvest gold, turquoise or green.

"Trim and baseboards can be strong features if they are more than 3 inches in height. Strengthen the appearance by contrasting their color with the surfaces against which they are placed."

"Bright white ceilings, which we believe are the norm, actually draw attention away from the objects in a space."

You are best to integrate these items into a scheme and make them a part of it. Don't ignore these pieces and attempt to decorate around them. You can't avoid them, but you can minimize them.

For instance, if you have brown bathroom fixtures, choose a color that helps to blend them in, to make them visually disappear. In this case, choose beige or brown as either wall colors or accents to make the bathroom fixtures blend in with their surroundings. Although they may be items you wish to hide, they will, unfortunately, dictate the color scheme.

A three-course meal of **color**

COLOR PLACEMENT

When selecting a color palette, there are three main categories to consider:
1. Background color
2. Foreground colors
3. Accent color

BACKGROUND COLOR

This is the color that will cover the majority of the room. It is the main color chosen to complement most of the fixed elements of the decor. For instance, if you have a wood floor in walnut brown, your wall and textile colors should complement this element. It is here that the choice of a warm or cool tone may be made. This choice will impact the selection of other colors within the space.

FOREGROUND COLORS

These colors are most prevalent in the furnishings of a room, including the sofa, chair, drapery, beds, rugs or carpeting. They are chosen to blend and complement the main colors of the space. Foreground colors have some of the main colors mixed among them for harmony, unless another effect is desired.

When selecting patterned or multi-colored objects for the foreground colors, remember that the room's main colors will emphasize one of the colors in your furnishings. For instance, if you have drapes with a sky-blue pattern, the color will be stronger against a blue wall, rather than a pink wall.

THE SPICE OF ACCENT COLORS

These are the colors that really bring a room to life. They are the splashes of color in objects, stencils, borders, lamps, photos or paintings that give punch to the main and foreground colors. They can be stronger and brighter than the overall room decor, but are used in smaller doses.

This is an excellent opportunity to make use of complementary colors. For example, Mediterranean blue adds vibrancy and warmth to a terra-cotta scheme; red punctuates the look of a room decorated in sage green; and plum adds pizzazz to yellow. These are effective as complements placed together, because they add visual energy to a space.

TRYING SOMETHING NEW

Although many of us strive for maximum impact when decorating a room, the stress of making a dramatic change can be overwhelming. Once a color has been applied to the wall, do not judge it immediately. Remember that if you have just finished painting, none of the objects that made the wall choice seem appropriate have been put back in place. Live with the color for at least seven days before you decide to change it. It takes time to adjust to a color change.

If you have lived in rooms that have been white for several years and then decide to add color to the walls, do not be shocked if the new color seems dark. All color choice is relative to the color with which it is being compared. Since you are covering white with a dark color, your eye will naturally perceive the color as darker than it actually is. Apply the color to all the walls, eliminating the white background, before you decide if the color is really too dark.

PICKY COLORS

Although a color can be made to work in almost any scheme, there are some colors that can be overwhelming and difficult to work with. Here are common problems that certain colors present:

Yellow

Be careful to select a slightly lighter yellow than you think you want, because it may appear very bright on the wall. Yellow has the highest reflective value of light. As a result, it appears brighter than other colors. Also: be careful when selecting a deep mustard yellow, because it can look somewhat green on a wall in fluorescent lighting.

Pink

Pink can be difficult, because it often appears much pinker on the wall than on a paint chip. If a dusty-rose color is desired, choose a pink with a gray tone, so you don't get the bubble-gum pink created by incandescent lighting.

Blue

Although blue is generally an easier color to select, if you choose a gray-blue, be sure it does not have too much black tint to it or it will look more gray than blue on the wall. To counteract this, select a blue with a yellow undertone, so that it maintains some brightness. When choosing periwinkle, be careful not to choose one with too much red in it – although it may appear pleasant on the small sample chip, on a wall, under warm lighting, the color may look more purple than blue.

Beige/taupe

Choose these colors carefully. Otherwise, they can look drab or dull when applied to the wall.

TRENDS

"To trend? Or not to trend?" That's the question! Color trends are often dictated by fashion and similar industries, but how realistic are they? A trend is a direction that lasts at least five to seven years, whereas a fad is much shorter in duration, lasting only six months to a year. Color trends are important to the fashion industry and those industries whose products use and sell color. After all, it is often the consumer's desire to try new colors that drives further sales.

Trend forecasting is done by private companies to launch future product lines, as well as by organizations consisting of many industry professionals. One such group is the Color Marketing Group, based in the U.S. This group has about 2,000 members from around the world. Members meet twice a year to predict trends in industries, from automotive to retail.

Color forecasting is usually predicted one to three years into the future. Trends are anticipated based on world events, such as the site of the Olympics, for example. The Olympics are a major influence because the host country, its culture and colors are broadcast all over the world to millions of people. Other influential events include economic changes, population shifts and such events as the new millennium.

The more complex our lives become, the simpler our tastes tend to be – hence the retro colors of times gone by. If you are uncomfortable choosing trendy colors, keep in mind that interior colors for homes are slower to change than home accessories, for example. Exterior colors stay popular for about seven years, so choose colors that have staying power.

To add trendy or *hip* colors to your home, select items that are relatively inexpensive, such as throw pillows, silk flowers, picture frames and tableware. Maintain basic colors for more expensive items and add dashes of color for interest. This way, you'll feel you're up-to-date with the trends, but not spending a lot of money making big changes.

The best place to experiment with trendy colors is with paint on the walls, because it is easy and inexpensive to change. New hot colors can change a room completely: a shot of trendy lime green, for example, will add a *hip* note to your design.

COLORS WITH STAYING POWER

When choosing expensive permanent items for your home, consider neutral colors. Neutrals include white, black, beige, almond, taupe, gray and silver. The benefit of choosing these colors for surfaces that you will not change frequently is that they tend to blend with most other colors and do not date as quickly.

For instance, choose beige tiles for a kitchen floor and hallway, if you want them to look good even when your tastes change. Large items, such as appliances and bathroom

The red-green complementary relationship is maintained when each color is made into a tint or shade. Complements, when viewed side by side, will intensify each other, even when their value is changed, although the intensity may be slightly diminished. From the top: a gray version of red and green; a tint of red and green; the full chroma of red and green; shades of red and green.

The yellow-and-purple complement relationship is the easiest to see, because of the clarity of these two colors. When white, black or gray are added to original full-intensity yellow or purple, they are still complements, but the strength of the relationship is not as intense. From the top: gray has been added to purple and yellow; white has been added to each color; the pure color; black has been added to each color.

Orange and blue are direct complements of each other and will continue to exhibit this unique relationship even when the original full chroma colors are changed. When tints and shades of colors are created from an original pure color, they make new colors, such as peach or terra-cotta. From the top: a blue and gray-orange; a tint of blue and a tint of orange; pure blue and orange; black has been added to blue and orange.

Imagine you finally receive this month's issue of your favorite decorating magazine and you choose a color from one of the featured decors. But when you select the paint-strip chip listed in the magazine, it doesn't look anything like the color in the picture. How disappointing!

This happens because the lighting used for photography changes the appearance of the paint color. Perhaps more significantly, however, is the change in color that occurs during the printing process of magazines. The colors of inks vary from publication to publication, as does the quality of paper on which the magazine is printed. As a result, a color can vary widely from its original chip. So, be sure to view a sample of the real paint color before you purchase a can.

fixtures, are also best left neutral, so that these permanent fixtures remain as background to exciting new colors added around them. As long as the more permanent items of the decor stay neutral, punch and excitement can come from accent colors.

CONQUERING FEAR

The most paralyzing, but consistent emotion many home decorators feel once decisions have been made is fear: fear they've made the wrong choice; fear of friends' and neighbors' reactions; and fear of change.

Once you have selected a common fabric, textile or style to be repeated in a variety of forms throughout your house, little can go wrong. Have faith. Do not show your friends or neighbors your choices until the work is done. After all, they probably don't have your vision!

LOOK AT THE WHOLE MENU

These steps will help you get started on your color choices:

1. Determine the furniture, materials and fixtures that you intend to keep in the room.

2. If at all possible, select any new major purchase at this time. If an item is on order, try to get a sample of its material. Don't trust your memory.

3. Look at pictures, samples, materials or colors for inspiration. This will help you to focus on your vision for the space.

4. Determine the lighting that is to be used, so you can get a feel for the function of the space.

5. Collect samples of your ideas and look at them together to decide your final choices. Once the items for the room have been set, look for common color themes.

6. Keep your pieces of inspiration with you when shopping for paint, so your vision stays fresh in your mind. An envelope or plastic sandwich bag works well to keep samples together.

7. Select a variety of paint chips in all possible color ranges, as determined by your samples. You can also choose colors that you may not like initially but which work with the scheme, and take them home.

8. Lay out all the samples and your paint chips in the room. Choose the chips you like best.

9. Study the combination of colors and materials under daytime and evening conditions to see how they change.

10. If you are still not sure of your color choice, get a larger sample of the paint chip so you can see it better and compare it with your samples again.

11. Just do it! Once the color has been decided, simply buy the amount you need and begin painting. You will never know if you like it if you don't put it on the wall.

Good-taste tip
IT'S IN THE CAN
Never judge a paint color by what's in the can or the wet paint on the lid. Paint always dries to a darker color than when it is wet.

When you decide to create *Room Recipe* styles in your home, these *Room Recipe Cards* will help you work smart and stay organized. On the front, you'll find everything you need to make the style work; on the back are actual color samples. You may want to clip out these cards and take them with you when you go shopping. You will find these cards a great time-saver when ordering paint and selecting accessories and furnishings.

MANOR HOUSE

INGREDIENTS
Add:

- Crown moldings
- Faux woodgrain
- Antique accents
- Warm walls
- A touch of class

SERVES UP: A CLASSIC READING ROOM

The look is sophisticated and formal, with rich colors and aged materials. This style embodies the manners and tradition of times gone by. It features collections of treasured heirlooms set against textured fabrics and balanced symmetry. Select this look to create a formal elegant room that will always be in style.

Benjamin Moore Paint Experts

COMPLETE RECIPE, PAGE 21
PAINT SAMPLES ON THE BACK

PROVENÇAL

INGREDIENTS
Add:

- Assorted patterns
- Aged textures
- Blue accents
- An old armoire
- A dash of "Dijon"

SERVES UP: A COUNTRY GUEST ROOM

This look is unpolished and features distressed wood. The airy style, reminiscent of the French countryside, is light in color but long on style. Blues, yellows and whites, combined with red and green accents, define this casual style.

Benjamin Moore Paint Experts

COMPLETE RECIPE, PAGE 27
PAINT SAMPLES ON THE BACK

These are the actual colors used to create each of the *Room Recipe* styles; many are from the **Regal Signature Color Collection**. A special printing process was needed to do full justice to their richness and intensity.

In fact, a new approach to paint formulation and application was required to make colors of this kind possible. Many are mixed with a new clear tinting base, which sets new standards for clarity and depth of color. Benjamin Moore also developed a special tinted *Regal FirstCoat* which is essential for the development of full color values.

As a result, most Signature Colors require one FirstCoat and two top coats to achieve their full value. Do not be concerned if the earlier coats are not as shown here. Only after each coat is applied and the process is complete, will the final fully saturated color appear.

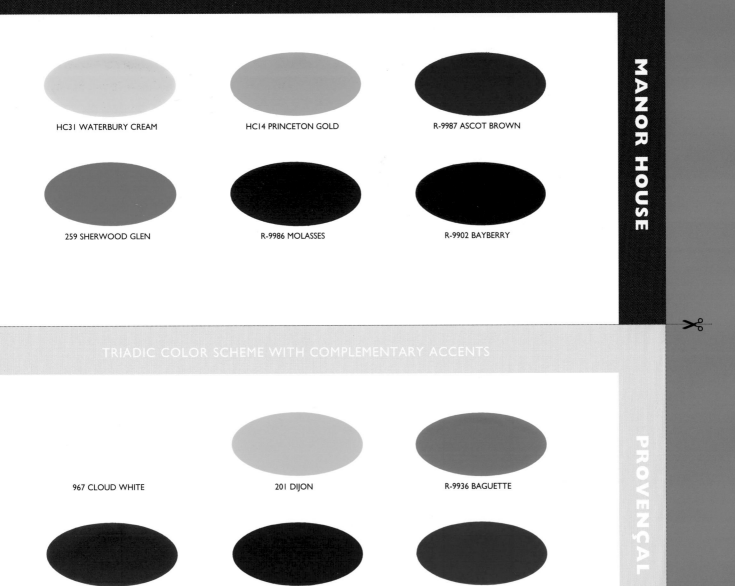

COMPLEMENTARY COLOR SCHEME WITH NEUTRALS

HC31 WATERBURY CREAM

HC14 PRINCETON GOLD

R-9987 ASCOT BROWN

259 SHERWOOD GLEN

R-9986 MOLASSES

R-9902 BAYBERRY

MANOR HOUSE

TRIADIC COLOR SCHEME WITH COMPLEMENTARY ACCENTS

967 CLOUD WHITE

201 DIJON

R-9936 BAGUETTE

R-9911 LYONS RED

R-9958 ANISETTE

R-9953 ARIES GREEN

PROVENÇAL

PACIFIC IMPRESSIONS

INGREDIENTS
Add:

- A wood border
- Dark trim
- Light wood
- Asian accents
- A hint of red

SERVES UP: A PEACEFUL BATHROOM

This look is simple, quiet, strong and linear. Drift to the Far East to capture some of the controlled calm of this Pacific style. Its unswerving exactness and linear organization bring grace to any room — even a bathroom.

Benjamin Moore
Paint Experts

COMPLETE RECIPE, PAGE 33
PAINT SAMPLES ON THE BACK

TAILORED CLASSICS

INGREDIENTS
Add:

- Subtle texture
- Masculine flavor
- Velvet accents
- A touch of shine

SERVES UP: A MODERN MASTER BEDROOM

This look is restrained, tailored, modern and strong — with timeless style. It will fit anywhere the desired look is clean and uncluttered.

Benjamin Moore
Paint Experts

COMPLETE RECIPE, PAGE 37
PAINT SAMPLES ON THE BACK

NORDIC NEUTRALS

INGREDIENTS
Add:

- Shades of white
- Potted plants
- Soft fabrics
- Textured walls
- Icy Accents

SERVES UP: A COOL MASTER BATH

This cool-colored room reflects the light, but strong nature of Scandinavian style. It is neat and highly styled, as well as functional and practical.

Benjamin Moore
Paint Experts

COMPLETE RECIPE, PAGE 43
PAINT SAMPLES ON THE BACK

MONOCHROMATIC COLOR SCHEME WITH COMPLEMENTARY ACCENTS

436 LEMON GRASS

R-9912 PAGODA

R-9940 BONSAI

MONOCHROMATIC COLOR SCHEME WITH ACCENTS

R-9990 ASPHALT

R-9961 BLUE SERGE

R-9993 TURRET

1542 HABERDASHER GRAY

1037 MUSLIN

MONOCHROMATIC COLOR SCHEME WITH ACCENTS

973 DANISH PEWTER

1629 BACHELOR BLUE

R-9992 NORDIC GRAY

R-9999 NORWEGIAN WOOD

967 CLOUD WHITE

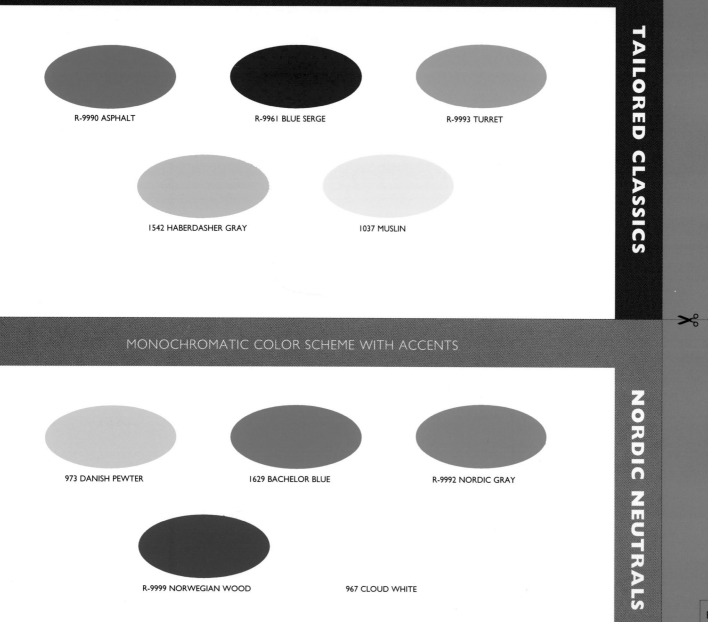

INGREDIENTS
Add:

- Bright fabrics
- Handpainted art
- Neutral furniture
- 4 wall colors
- A dab of white

SERVES UP: A BRIGHT BEDROOM

Add punch to a room with paint – while being practical! Apply color only to the surfaces that are easily changed, while retaining the natural or neutral colors of more permanent items.

Benjamin Moore Paint Experts

COMPLETE RECIPE, PAGE 47
PAINT SAMPLES ON THE BACK

INGREDIENTS
Add:

- Cream walls
- Aged wainscoting
- 4 colorful towels
- 2 round mirrors
- A touch of orange

SERVES UP: A PERFECT POWDER ROOM

This look is sun-drenched, casual, relaxed and easy. It is a wonderful light style that is harmonious with water, washed materials and sun-drenched surfaces. Add beach trinkets to the design for some fun and color – after all, life's a beach!

Benjamin Moore Paint Experts

COMPLETE RECIPE, PAGE 51
PAINT SAMPLES ON THE BACK

INGREDIENTS
Add:

- A touch of gold
- Rich patterns
- Faux blocks
- Warm colors
- One tapestry

SERVES UP: A CLASSICAL HALLWAY

A style that comes from a time gone by, this look captures the aged finishes of the relics we see today. Although this is a look that appears to have aged through time, you can capture its air of elegant decay today.

Benjamin Moore Paint Experts

COMPLETE RECIPE, PAGE 55
PAINT SAMPLES ON THE BACK

RR5

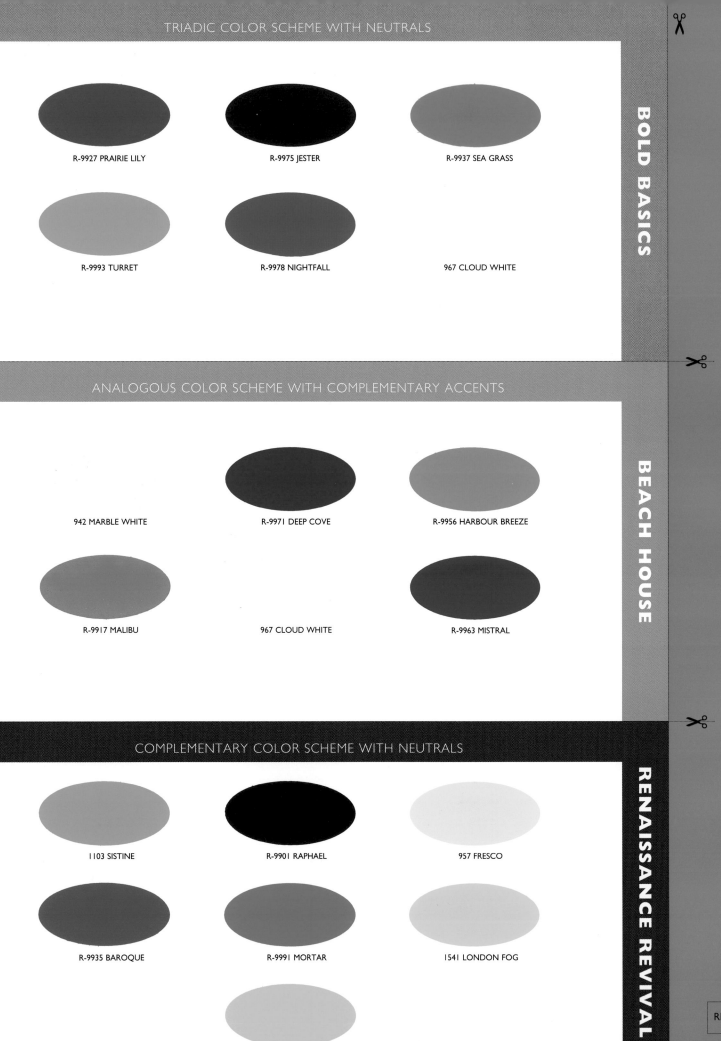

TRIADIC COLOR SCHEME WITH NEUTRALS

R-9927 PRAIRIE LILY

R-9975 JESTER

R-9937 SEA GRASS

R-9993 TURRET

R-9978 NIGHTFALL

967 CLOUD WHITE

ANALOGOUS COLOR SCHEME WITH COMPLEMENTARY ACCENTS

942 MARBLE WHITE

R-9971 DEEP COVE

R-9956 HARBOUR BREEZE

R-9917 MALIBU

967 CLOUD WHITE

R-9963 MISTRAL

COMPLEMENTARY COLOR SCHEME WITH NEUTRALS

1103 SISTINE

R-9901 RAPHAEL

957 FRESCO

R-9935 BAROQUE

R-9991 MORTAR

1541 LONDON FOG

976 FLORENTINE PLASTER

BOLD BASICS

BEACH HOUSE

RENAISSANCE REVIVAL

RR6

INGREDIENTS
Add:

- Rich browns
- Light neutrals
- Soft textures
- Tailored furniture
- Wood accents

SERVES UP: A NATURAL LIVING & DINING ROOM

It is possible to add depth and interest to a space with little color. Just ensure that you have a good mix of textures and different values of your neutral tones. This look has clean lines and is free of ornamentation, but is rich with subtle pattern, sheen and texture.

Benjamin Moore
Paint Experts

COMPLETE RECIPE, PAGE 61
PAINT SAMPLES ON THE BACK

GARDEN PORTFOLIO

INGREDIENTS
Add:

- Crackle finishes
- An old screen door
- Painted paneling
- Sunflowers
- A dash of ingenuity

SERVES UP: A GARDEN-INSPIRED OFFICE

A clean, but comfortable style, this look capitalizes on the natural beauty of greenery within the home. Touches of color are evident in the florals, but the palette is a fresh collection of shades from nature. Forms are elementary, while the style is practical – with the earthy feel of a country potting shed.

Benjamin Moore
Paint Experts

COMPLETE RECIPE, PAGE 67
PAINT SAMPLES ON THE BACK

MEDITERRANEAN BREEZE

INGREDIENTS
Add:

- Faux tiles
- Bright colors
- Iron accents
- A dash of texture
- A collection of candles

SERVES UP: A SPICY KITCHEN

This look is graphic, clean, bold and simple. Strong colors, such as cool blues and warm reds and yellows, are placed against each other for contrast. Add spice to any space with this citrus-and-cypress Mediterranean styling.

Benjamin Moore
Paint Experts

COMPLETE RECIPE, PAGE 73
PAINT SAMPLES ON THE BACK

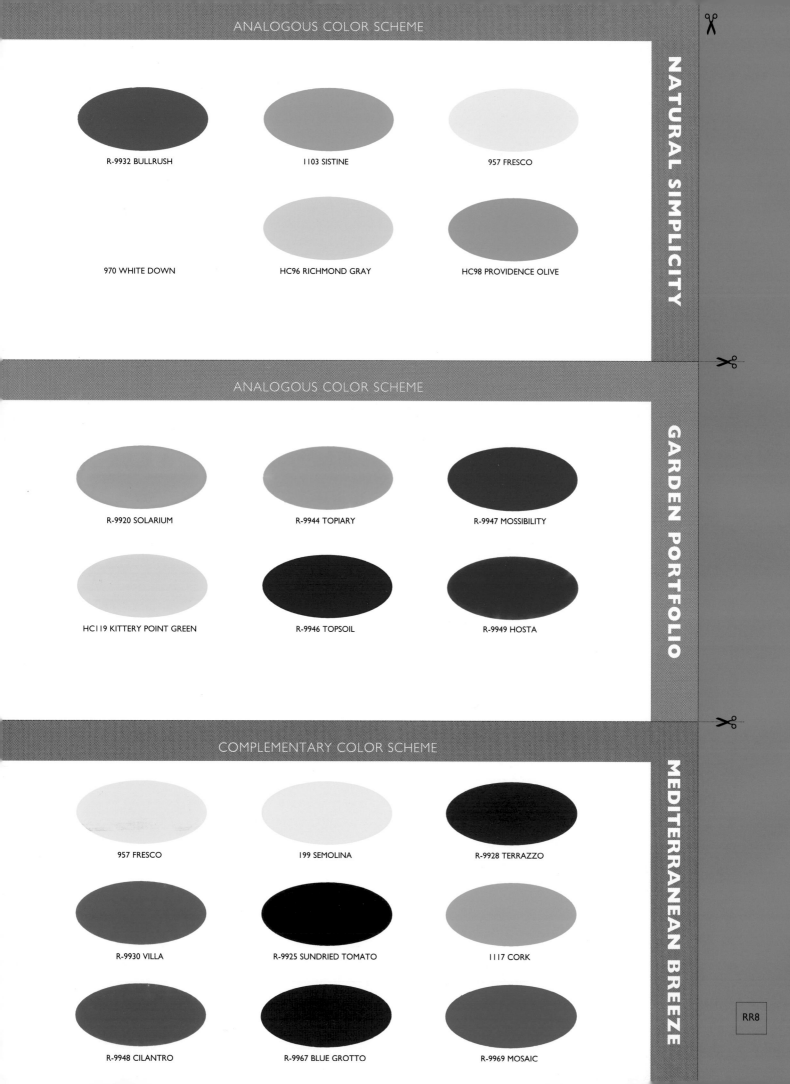

ANALOGOUS COLOR SCHEME

R-9932 BULLRUSH

1103 SISTINE

957 FRESCO

970 WHITE DOWN

HC96 RICHMOND GRAY

HC98 PROVIDENCE OLIVE

ANALOGOUS COLOR SCHEME

R-9920 SOLARIUM

R-9944 TOPIARY

R-9947 MOSSIBILITY

HC119 KITTERY POINT GREEN

R-9946 TOPSOIL

R-9949 HOSTA

COMPLEMENTARY COLOR SCHEME

957 FRESCO

199 SEMOLINA

R-9928 TERRAZZO

R-9930 VILLA

R-9925 SUNDRIED TOMATO

1117 CORK

R-9948 CILANTRO

R-9967 BLUE GROTTO

R-9969 MOSAIC

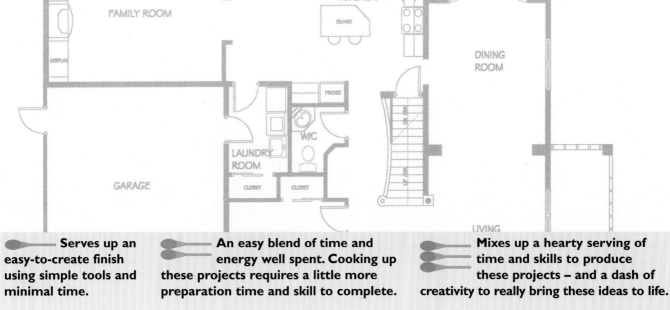

CHAPTER THREE

Room **recipes**

Choosing colors is much easier if you can decide on a design style first. This can range from identifying a simple monochromatic scheme to creating an entire French-country environment.

Choices depend on your likes and dislikes, your needs and desires. Often, we inherently know the style we like and can describe it with great passion. But achieving that look can be frustrating. Perhaps the most difficult aspect is selecting the appropriate colors, because the slightest change in tone can produce a different look.

A color palette, ranging from the spicy warm tones of the Mediterranean to the icy cool neutrals of Scandinavia, can help you determine the design style you desire. It is color that often defines a space, even before the other details enhance it.

This chapter introduces 11 *Room Recipes* to showcase specific styles. You will find special color palettes, in the form of recipe cards for each look, following Chapter Two. Follow the recipe exactly to achieve the style, or add a dash of your own ingredients to create a unique *Room Recipe*.

Serves up an easy-to-create finish using simple tools and minimal time.

An easy blend of time and energy well spent. Cooking up these projects requires a little more preparation time and skill to complete.

Mixes up a hearty serving of time and skills to produce these projects – and a dash of creativity to really bring these ideas to life.

The rich tones of the Manor House room are complemented by dark furniture and traditional accessories.

The look is sophisticated and formal, with rich colors and aged materials. This style embodies the manners and tradition of times gone by. It features collections of treasured heirlooms set against textured fabrics and balanced symmetry. Select this look to create a formal elegant room that will always be in style.

COMPLEMENTARY COLOR SCHEME WITH NEUTRALS

SECRET INGREDIENTS

- Use dark rich colors,.
- Integrate Old English motifs into fabrics and furniture.
- Include at least one leather furnishing or accessory.
- Add old books and accessorize with an old clock or maps.
- Choose large furniture for a smaller space to give the room a cozy feel.
- Incorporate the colors, styles and motifs of the fox hunt and other sporting pastimes.

COLOR MENU

Ceiling
Wall Satin, Waterbury Cream HC31

Trim
AquaPearl, Ascot Brown R-9987

Wall base
AquaPearl, Princeton Gold HC14

Leather
AquaPearl, Bayberry R-9902
Molasses R-9986

Dry brush
AquaVelvet, Sherwood Glen 259

STYLE A LA CARTE

Furniture and accessories courtesy of: Bamboo blinds, IKEA/Armchair, area carpet, tray table, leather sofa, wall pictures, ELTE CARPETS & HOME/ Chest with doors, desk, MARY DOBSON/Desk chair, plant stand, NANCY LOCKHART/Crown molding, ceiling medallion, BALMER STUDIOS.

PAINT TECHNIQUE:

LEATHER WAINSCOTING

This technique is an easy way to create the look of old leather wainscoting in a library or den.

INGREDIENTS

2-inch painter's tape (delicate)
9½-inch roller and tray
Plastic drop sheet (medium-density)
Paintbrush
Level
Tape measure
Upholstery tacks (aged brass)
Gloves

PAINT

Base coat
AquaPearl, Bayberry R-9902

Faux leather
5 parts AquaGlaze to 1 part AquaPearl, Molasses R-9986

PREPARATION

1. Apply tape 36 inches above the floor surface. Make sure the line is level.
2. Apply the base coat within this area and allow it to dry.
3. Mix the glaze and roll on wall from the top of the level line to the baseboard, in an area approximately 5 feet wide. Tape off this section to create panels and seams where they come together.
4. Use an unfolded plastic drop sheet and press over top of wet glaze, smoothing it out with your hand.

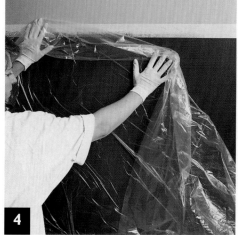

5. Repeat steps 3 and 4 on all the walls of the room and allow glaze to dry.
6. To finish the look of the leather, add upholstery tacks about 1 inch apart along the vertical seams of the wainscoting, all the way around the room.
7. Add the chair rail 36 inches above the floor, once the wall is dry.

PAINT TECHNIQUE:
WOODGRAIN TRIM

To create a simple woodgrain look, use this technique on baseboards, trim and doors.

INGREDIENTS

2½-inch angled bristle sash brush

Bucket

Stir stick

Lint-free rag

Gloves

PAINT

Base coat

AquaPearl, Waterbury Cream HC31

Woodgrain coat

1 part Stays Clear high-gloss latex urethane to 1 part AquaPearl, Ascot Brown R-9987

PREPARATION

1. Apply the base coat to the wood and allow it to dry.

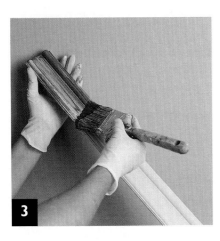

2. Pour equal amounts of paint and urethane into a bucket and stir together.

3. Begin brushing mixture onto the trim, covering about 4 lineal feet at a time.

4. Remove the excess paint from the brush by wiping it onto a rag. Take the brush and drag it horizontally through the wet paint, creating a linear pattern. Continue to brush the same area until the desired look is reached.

5. Repeat along the rest of the trim. Remember to work quickly, as the mixture dries fast.

6. For a high-gloss finish, recoat with clear urethane.

PAINT TECHNIQUE:
DRY-BRUSH STRIPES

This elegant and inexpensive technique mimics the look of sophisticated wallpaper – without the cost.

INGREDIENTS

2-inch painter's tape (delicate)

2½-inch paintbrush

Level

Tape measure

Cardboard

Gloves

PAINT

Base coat

AquaPearl, Princeton Gold HC14

Decorative stripe coat

AquaVelvet, Sherwood Glen 259

Wash coat

1 part AquaPearl, Princeton Gold HC14 mixed with 1 part water and 1 part AquaGlaze

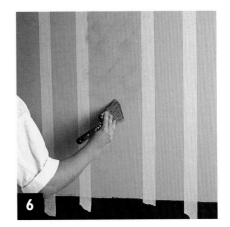

PREPARATION

1. Apply the base coat 36 inches above the floor to the ceiling. Allow it to dry.

2. Beginning in the least visible corner, measure out 8 inches from the corner and draw a vertical line. On the left side of this line, apply tape from the ceiling to the top of the wainscoting.

3. Measure 8 inches from this line and apply a second line of tape from ceiling to wainscoting on the right side of the 8 inches. This ensures an 8-inch-wide stripe.

4. Continue to apply tape in this manner to create stripes around the room.

5. Dip the tip of the paintbrush into 259 and brush off a bit onto an extra piece of cardboard.

6. Apply the paint between the tape in a crosshatching manner. Repeat down the length of each stripe.

7. Allow it to dry and remove the tape.

8. Optional: to soften the final look, apply a wash coat (1 part water to 1 part paint) of the base color over the full surface with a rag and allow it to dry.

9. Repeat on the remaining walls.

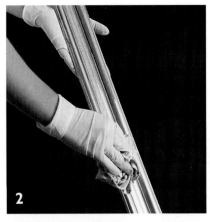

2

PAINT TECHNIQUE:

ANTIQUING TRIM

This technique offers a quick way to age moldings, trim and doors in gold or silver.

INGREDIENTS

Paintbrush

Bucket of water

Rags

Gloves

PAINT

Base paint

Utilac gold spray paint

Glaze

5 parts AquaGlaze to 1 part AquaPearl, Ascot Brown R-9987

PREPARATION

1. Spray the molding with gold paint; this should be done in a well-ventilated area before installation. Allow it to dry.

2. Using a brush, add the glaze color to the molding. Before it dries, wipe away the excess with a rag, pushing the glaze into the relief. Allow it to dry and install.

3. Follow the same procedure on the trim and doors.

NOTE:

This is easiest to do on trim or molding that has some relief or a design, as it takes the glaze better.

Polyurethane crown molding is painted gold and antiqued to complement the cream ceiling and golden yellow walls. The molding also picks up the gilt of the picture frame and accessories.

"Crown molding is a feature that enhances the appearance of a room, yet few people give this wonderful feature the attention it deserves."

Plain rectangular windows take on the look of an English manor house with an arched wood header and flowing tapestry drapes.

The faux-leather wainscoting on the wall is completed with upholstery tacks. The detailing is carried over to the traditional English leather sofa.

The gold ceiling ornamentation enhances the Old English feeling of the room and adds a striking decorative detail.

"The light in a room may appear less strong when a dark color is on the wall, because the dark color absorbs more light."

WINDOW DRESSING:

STATIONARY PANELS DISPLAYED
OVER AN ARCHED VALANCE

(Size: 95 inches x 40 inches)

INGREDIENTS

¼-inch Masonite

3 feet (1-inch x 2-inch) pine

Fabric:

• 5 meters Enniskillen, color Burgundy
(allow extra fabric for pattern
matching)

• 5½ meters lining (optional)

3 meters Velcro™ shirring tape

1 meter hard-sided Velcro

3 (2-inch) L-brackets

4 drapery weights

PREPARATION

1. Create an arched valance box
   with the center 5 inches higher
   than the sides. Cut it out of the
   Masonite.

2. Center the 1-inch x 2-inch pine at
   the back of the arch, with the
   1-inch side against the Masonite.
   Screw in from the front. Paint the
   board to coordinate and stencil, if
   desired. Be sure to fill in screw
   heads and paint. Cut 2 lengths of
   fabric 54 inches x 106 inches. Turn,
   press and stitch a double 4-inch
   hem. Turn, press and stitch a
   double 1 inch hem down both
   sides of each panel. Tack a weight
   inside the bottom corner of each.
   Mark 1 panel as the right side and
   the other as the left.

3. Mark down 5 inches from the top
   right on the right panel and at the
   top left on the left panel. Mark a
   diagonal line from the top
   opposite corner to the 5-inch
   mark on other side and cut. Turn
   the top edge 1-inch back and
   press flat.

4. Working at the back of the panel,
   place the shirring tape along the
   top folded edge and cut ½ inch
   longer at each end. Press the ends
   of the tape under and stitch.

5. Gather a total width of 20 inches.
   Cut the hard-sided Velcro into 2
   (20-inch) sections and staple to
   the top edge of the arch. Measure
   from the center top of the arch to
   the underside of the pine board.
   Add ½ inch and measure down
   from the ceiling, marking for the
   placement of the brackets. Place
   the brackets in a level line, 1 in the
   center and the others 1¼ inches
   away on either side. Place the arch
   (pine board) on top of the
   brackets and screw it in from
   below to secure it. Place the
   gathered panels onto the Velcro
   and fan the outside corners, so
   that they wrap around the
   corners of the arch.

"Dark colors do not
make a room look
smaller. Rather, it is
the contrast that
makes a room
appear smaller."

The flavor of the French countryside is captured in this bedroom, with its rich painted ceiling, aged walls and decorative woven carpet. White, yellow and blue are the dominant colors in the room. Delicate white accessories help to create a light airy look, while the daybed turns the space into an inviting sitting room.

PROVENÇAL: BEDROOM

This look is unpolished and features distressed wood. The airy style, reminiscent of the French countryside, is light in color, but long on style. Blues, yellows and whites, combined with red and green accents, define this casual style.

TRIADIC COLOR SCHEME WITH COMPLEMENTARY ACCENTS

- Do not match color and fabric perfectly.

- Add handmade elements, such as quilts.

- Add old weathered furniture.

- Start with a blue, white and yellow color scheme, but accent with red and green.

COLOR MENU

Walls
AquaPearl, Cloud White 967

Ceiling
Wall Satin, Dijon 201

Trim
AquaPearl, Baguette R-9936

Dry brush
AquaPearl, Cloud White 967

Wall design
AquaPearl, Anisette R-9958

STYLE A LA CARTE

Furniture and accessories courtesy of: Wicker chest, day bed, bowl and pitcher, curtain tie backs (as door knobs), crystal finials (as door handles), IKEA/Area carpet ELTE CARPETS & HOME/Lavender, napkins, vintage books, lace in armoire, PUTTI FINE FURNISHINGS/Chairs, quilts, wall plates, wall pictures, MARY DOBSON.

PAINT TECHNIQUE:

PAINTED PROVENÇAL PRINT

This diamond-pattern paint technique uses simple tools and gives color and design to an otherwise plain wall.

INGREDIENTS

Utility knife

Straight edge

Pencil

Extra cardboard

Illustration art board

Tape

3-inch high-density foam roller and tray

Gloves

Hot glue

Mylar

PAINT

Base paint

AquaPearl, Cloud White 967

Diamonds
AquaPearl, Anisette R-9958

Center stencil
AquaPearl, Baguette R-9936

Trim
AquaPearl, Baguette R-9936
Cloud White 967

Ceiling
AquaPearl, Dijon 201

PREPARATION

1. Apply base coat to the wall and allow it to dry completely.

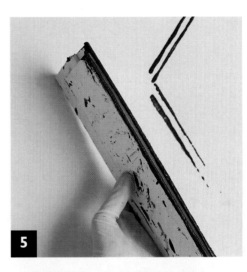

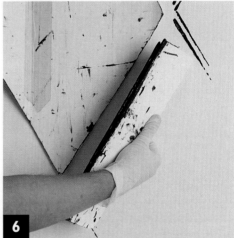

2. Measure the overall height of the wall from floor to ceiling. Determine the vertical size you want for each diamond.

3. On the piece of illustration art board, measure out the size of the diamond and cut out. Add some extra cardboard to the back of the diamond to make a handle or grip, if desired.

Before

This old armoire was refurbished in the French-country style with the addition of crown molding, interior shelves and white chicken wire on the doors. For antique flare, the finish was aged by sanding the edges.

7

8

1 part water over top to soften, if desired, before applying the stencil. Cut your own stencil out of Mylar to fit onto the adjoining points of the painted diamond pattern. Place stencil and roll paint lightly over top.

9. Complete across the wall until finished.

PAINT TECHNIQUE:

GINGHAM DOOR

This unique door detail lends grace and style to any plain door.

INGREDIENTS

Painter's tape

3-inch high-density foam roller and tray

Tape measure

Utility knife

Pencil

Small paintbrush

Gloves

PAINT

Base color

AquaPearl, Cloud White 967

Gingham paint

1 part AquaGlaze to 1 part AquaPearl, Anisette R-9958

PREPARATION

1. Apply base paint to the door and allow it to dry.

2. Using a pencil, divide a 3-inch foam roller into 3 equal sections. Apply tape to the right and left side of the middle section of the roller.

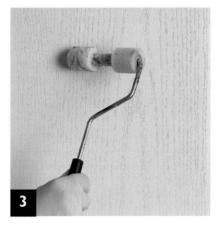

3

5

3. With a utility knife, cut out the middle section of the foam roller.

4. Mix glaze and paint together. Apply mixture to the roller and roll onto the surface in a vertical line. Continue lines down the surface, leaving equal distance between each set of stripes. Allow paint to dry, once the vertical stripes are complete.

5. Repeat the same procedure with the cut roller, but roll in a horizontal direction to create a gingham look. Complete the surface and then allow it to dry.

6. Where the horizontal and vertical stripes overlap, paint a darker square over top to complete the look of gingham, if desired.

4. Start in the corner that's least visible from the door. Place the cardboard diamond against the wall and mark the points. Tape the cardboard diamond in position for the first painted diamond. Use a level to check that the top and bottom points of the diamond are level.

5. Create the *paint tool* with 2 lengths of illustration art board, sized to match the length of 1 side of the diamond. Sandwich and glue a piece of foam core between the 2 lengths of illustration art board, creating 2 parallel lines. Be sure that at least 1 face of the cardboard tool has 2 flush surfaces.

6. Dip the *paint tool* into a pool of paint. Dab off on extra cardboard. Apply paint to the wall, following the edges of the diamond taped in place.

7. Complete this pattern across the wall. Allow it to dry.

8. Add a wash of 1 part 967 and

A small sitting area is created with the addition of a skirted table and painted chairs.
The table covering matches the drapery fabric, while the white lace overlay adds a country touch.

"Is it a room for peace and quiet?
Function determines the fixtures and furnishings
needed – whether your decor style is modern,
traditional, eclectic or country."

The sheer overlay softens the rich blue of the printed damask panel drapes, adding to the light airy feel of the room. The wooden rod and rings are painted white, then highlighted with gold spray paint for an antiqued finish.

WINDOW DRESSING:

DRAPES WITH SHEER OVERLAY

(Size: 40 inches x 96 inches)

INGREDIENTS

Fabric:

- 5½ meters Holice, color Lapis (allow extra for pattern matching)
- 0.7 meters (118-inch) sheers
- 5½ meters lining

4 drapery weights

3 meters wide shirring tape

Decorative rod and rings

Drapery hooks

PREPARATION

1. Cut 2 widths of fabric each to the length of the finished drape (96 inches) plus 9 inches. Turn, press and stitch a double 4-inch hem. From the sheers, cut two sections each the same width as the main fabric and 24 inches in length. Turn and press a double ½-inch hem along the bottom. Place the sheer wrong-side down on the right side of the main fabric, aligning the side and top edges. Working with both layers together, turn and press a double 1-inch hem along each side.

2. Measure the lining to 100 inches. Trim the width of the lining to the pressed width of the main fabric. Turn, press and stitch a double 3-inch hem on the lining. Place the lining on the main fabric, wrong-sides together, placing the cut edges under the pressed side hems. Bottom and top edges of the lining should both be 1 inch away from their corresponding edge of the main fabric. Stitch the side hems. Tack drapery weights inside each bottom corner.

3. Turn the top edge of the curtain to the back 1 inch and press. Cut the shirring tape 2 inches wider than the curtain. Align the top edges and fold under the ends of the tape. Stitch along the top edge of the tape between every row of gathering cords and along the bottom edge. Gather the curtain down to 20 inches. Insert drapery hooks at even intervals at the back of the curtain.

Closet-door pulls were created from decorative finials, which were screwed into the door to give the appearance of antique crystal door knobs. Hand-painted leaf detailing adds a pretty feminine touch.

Good-taste tip
BACK AWAY FROM THE WALL!
Don't hold a small paint chip against the wall to be painted, because the color behind the chip influences its appearance.

This Asian-inspired bathroom features cool green walls and dark-green accents, enhanced with a balsa-wood border and birch vanity. Curly willow branches, natural river stones and a bold floor mat add to the Far Eastern flavor of the room.

PACIFIC IMPRESSIONS: MAIN BATHROOM

This look is simple, quiet, strong and linear. Drift to the Far East to capture some of the controlled calm of this Pacific style. Its unswerving exactness and linear organization brings grace to any room – even a bathroom.

MONOCHROMATIC COLOR SCHEME WITH COMPLEMENTARY ACCENTS

SECRET INGREDIENTS

- Use light woods and natural ingredients.
- Keep space clutter-free.
- Concentrate on creating harmony and balance among objects in the room.
- Follow linear (vertical and horizontal) directions.
- Use peaceful color punctuated with small accents of bright red and orange.
- Think symmetry.

COLOR MENU
Walls
AquaPearl, Lemon Grass 436

Ceiling
AquaPearl, Bonsai R-9940

Carpet accent
AquaPearl, Pagoda R-9912

STYLE A LA CARTE
Furniture and accessories courtesy of: Towel ring, UMBRA/Shelves, KEN BALCER/Lights, IKEA.

PAINT TECHNIQUE:
VINYL FLOOR MAT
This project is an easy way to create a floor mat in any shape or size.

INGREDIENTS
Vinyl sheet flooring

Utility knife

Sandpaper and/or palm sander

T.S.P. or M-83

2½-inch angled sash paintbrush

9½-inch roller and tray

Dust mask

Gloves

1-inch foam brush

PAINT
Primer
Fresh Start Super Adherent Latex Primer

Base paint
Center: AquaPearl, Bonsai R-9940
Edge: AquaPearl, Pagoda R-9912

Stencil paint
Artist's water-based gold paint

Top coat
Stays Clear high-gloss latex urethane

PREPARATION

1. Determine the design and shape of your floor mat. For a circle, decide on the diameter you desire and find an object around your home that is close in size (such as a garbage-can base or lid).

2. Trace the design onto the vinyl sheet and cut it out with the utility knife.

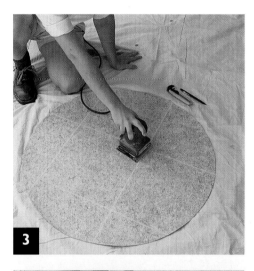

3. Sand the surface with the sandpaper or the palm sander. Wash with T.S.P. and rinse with water.

4. Apply the primer and allow it to dry.

5. Apply the base coat and allow it to dry.

6. First, draw the design onto the mat with

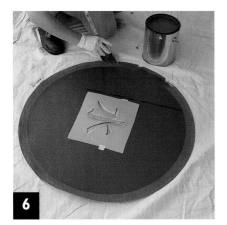

6

pencil. Then paint and allow it to dry. Or you may opt to cut a stencil of your design.

7. Apply 3 coats of urethane to the whole mat. (Be sure to use a non-skid mat underneath to ensure it won't slide on tiles.)

NOTE:

Don't let the mat sit in water for any length of time; always wipe up water quickly for long-lasting durability.

PROJECT:

BALSA-WOOD BORDER

This unique border integrates color and wood to create a three-dimensional design with the flavor of the Orient.

INGREDIENTS

Balsa wood of various thicknesses

Rag

Hot glue gun

Mylar

1-inch paintbrush

Tape measure

Knife

Gloves

PAINT

Wood coat

Utilac clear spray urethane

Stencil paint

Water-based artist's gold stencil paint

Ceiling color

AquaPearl, Bonsai R-9940

PREPARATION

1. On paper, decide what the border will look like.

2. In a well-ventilated area, spray wood pieces completely with Utilac clear spray and allow them to dry.

3. With a utility knife, cut all the pieces required to create the border to length. Measure and locate on the wall where the first vertical strips will go.

4. With hot glue, attach the first vertical pieces to the wall just below the ceiling. Allow to dry in place. Secure with tape, if necessary, to hold in place while glue is drying.

5. Apply second pieces of balsa to the first ones and secure with glue. Again, support with tape while glue dries, if necessary. Repeat until border is complete.

6. Draw and cut out the stencil design from a sheet of Mylar. Position stencil in every third open square of wood border. Apply gold

5

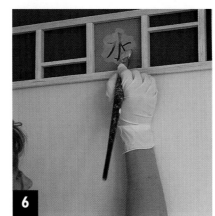

6

paint on top with the paintbrush.

7. Allow it to dry.

OPTIONAL:

Assemble border on floor first, then apply to wall completed. Secure with hot glue.

Here, natural balsa wood frames the dark painted ceiling, as well as a standard wall-mounted mirror. Sandblasted glass pendant lamps hang over the vanity to provide both light and a touch of Asian style.

The sheer printed fabric of the shower curtain, hung floor to ceiling, is topped by a continuation of the wood border. Balsa wood is also used to frame the plastic ceiling-fan cover, making it part of the room's design.

Double corner windows are treated with a dark-green panel behind fitted gathered sheers similar to the shower curtain. This simple design maintains the shape of the window, while adding softness and diffusing sunlight.

WINDOW DRESSING:

FLAT VALANCE UNDER
GATHERED SHEERS
(Size: 30 inches x 55 inches)

FLAT VALANCE

INGREDIENTS
Fabric:

- 1 meter Esashie, color Fern
- 1.5 meters sheer Palona, color Nugget

2 drapery weights

2 tension rods

PREPARATION

1. Measure the flat width of the inside of the window casing and add 2 inches for seam allowances. To determine the finished length, divide the length of the window in half for a short window or slightly longer than one-third for a tall window. Add 1 inch for bottom seam allowance and 2 inches for the top pocket. Cut a rectangle to these dimensions. Fold in half, then draw a diagonal line, beginning at its lowest point at the center fold and its highest point 8 inches up on the selvage edge. Repeat with

a second layer of the same fabric or of lining.

2. Place the 2 sections of fabric right-sides together. Sew a 1-inch seam down each side and each half of the bottom angle. Pivot the needle at each corner to avoid stretching the fabric as you sew along the angled seams. Trim the seams to ⅜ inch and clip across each of the corners. Flip right-side out and press flat. Turn and press the top edge to the back ½ inch and again 1½ inches. Stitch along the bottom fold edge only.

GATHERED SHEERS

PREPARATION

1. Measure the flat width of the inside of the window casing and multiply by 2 or 2½ to determine the fullness required. Measure the height of the window inside the casing and add 6 inches for the bottom hem and 2 inches for the top casing.

2. Turn and stitch a double 1-inch hem along each side edge. Tack drapery weights inside the bottom corners. Turn the top and bottom edges to the back 1 inch and press, then turn back 1½ inches again. Stitch along the bottom fold only, through all layers. Gather onto the tension rods and position in front of the first rod.

This simple, custom-built shelving unit provides the ideal space to display decorative items in the bathroom. The natural wood color blends well with the balsa-wood border.

Good-taste tip
NOW YOU SEE IT, NOW YOU DON'T
To make an object, such as an unsightly air vent, disappear, paint it the same or similar color as the wall behind it. To make an object, such as crown molding, stand out, paint it in a contrasting color to the surface against which it is placed.

The menswear-inspired color palette of this master bedroom creates a sophisticated cool atmosphere. The mood is enhanced by black furniture, gray sheets, strong blue accents and silver accessories. Shadow blocking on the wall adds subtle texture and drama to the room.

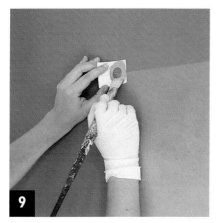
9

7. Repeat on each taped square.

8. Delicately remove the tape from the wall and allow it to dry.

9. At the intersection of each square, apply a stencil cut in the shape of a circle. This should be the size of a 25-cent piece. Apply silver metallic paint in the stencil and allow it to dry. Repeat at each intersection.

PAINT TECHNIQUE:

GLOSS WASH

A conservative, but high-fashion look can be created with this technique, using a rag and paint.

PAINT

Base paint

AquaVelvet, Asphalt R-9990

Gloss coat

Stays Clear high-gloss latex urethane

Wash color

1 part AquaPearl, Haberdasher Gray 1542 to 1 part water to 1 part AquaGlaze

3

INGREDIENTS

9½-inch roller and tray

Rag

Gloves

Bucket

Stir stick

PREPARATION

1. Tape off an area approximately 20 inches to 24 inches wide at eye level. Roll 1 coat of high-gloss latex urethane onto area and allow to dry.

2. Mix equal parts 1542, water and AquaGlaze in a bucket.

3. Dip rag in bucket and begin to wash over urethaned area, moving in a circular motion. Try to eliminate wash lines (the gloss underneath will help to prevent this).

4. Continue this process around the room and let dry.

A coating of silver spray paint helps tie an old brass-colored bench to the room's elegant silver accessories.

Panel tab drapes created from bright-blue and silver-gray fabrics follow the painted band around the bedroom. The blue of the fabric is brought up to the crown molding with the addition of a painted blue stripe.

Good-taste tip
A STEP UP
If you are fearful of applying a color that might be too dark overall, then select the same color one shade above, or higher, on the sample chip strip. This way, you will maintain the depth of color, but without as much intensity.

WINDOW DRESSING:

TAB CURTAINS

(Size: 40 inches x 96 inches)

INGREDIENTS
Fabric:

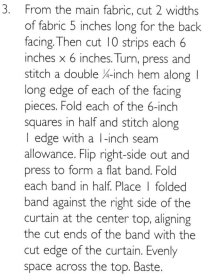

- 5½ meters Empoli, color Navy
- 1 meter Eton, color Slate
- 5½ meters lining

4 drapery weights

Decorative rod

PREPARATION

1. Cut 2 widths of the main fabric to 68 inches. Cut 2 widths of the contrast fabric to 24 inches and 2 more widths of the main fabric to 14 inches. Place the large main fabric right sides-together with 1 layer of the contrast section, matching the cut top edge of the larger section with the bottom of the contrast. Stitch together with a 1-inch seam allowance. Trim the seam and overcast. Press the seam allowance downward. Next, place 1 layer of the smaller main-fabric piece right-sides together with the first contrast piece. Align the top edge of the contrast section with the cut bottom edge of the smaller piece. Stitch, trim and press as before.

2. Turn, press and stitch a double 4-inch hem (at the bottom of the panels). Turn and press double 1-inch hems along each side edge. Cut 2 widths of lining measuring 100 inches for the bottom hem. Turn, press and stitch a double 3-inch hem at the bottom of each section of lining. Trim the lining down to the pressed width of the panel. Fold the lining under the pressed side hems and position the bottom hem 1 inch above the bottom hem of the curtain. The top edges should be even. Stitch the side hems, tacking drapery weights inside each bottom corner.

3. From the main fabric, cut 2 widths of fabric 5 inches long for the back facing. Then cut 10 strips each 6 inches x 6 inches. Turn, press and stitch a double ¼-inch hem along 1 long edge of each of the facing pieces. Fold each of the 6-inch squares in half and stitch along 1 edge with a 1-inch seam allowance. Flip right-side out and press to form a flat band. Fold each band in half. Place 1 folded band against the right side of the curtain at the center top, aligning the cut ends of the band with the cut edge of the curtain. Evenly space across the top. Baste.

4. Center the facing right-sides together with the curtain. Turn and press under the excess width, ⅛ inch in from the edge of the curtain. Stitch. Flip the facing to the back and press flat. Stitch down either end of the facing.

"Private space is not part of the overall house flow. You can be more daring in private rooms."

This modern screen was built from three pieces of M.D.F. (medium density fiberboard), then spray-painted silver and detailed with washers and screws. It adds a pleasant reflective glow to an otherwise dark corner.

"Each texture picks up light and shadows differently to provide subtle color changes."

White, gray and beige define this Scandinavian-inspired bathroom. Washed walls, a white painted vanity and linear stencil work together to create a clean, icy-cool atmosphere. Natural greenery adds color and texture to the room.

NORDIC NEUTRALS: MASTER BATHROOM

This cool-colored room reflects the light, but strong nature of Scandinavian style.
It is neat and highly styled, as well as functional and practical.

MONOCHROMATIC COLOR SCHEME WITH ACCENTS

- Select a variety of whites, including blue and yellow-based whites.

- Add strong lines in furniture and accessories, but use light colors.

- Pick old, weathered or whitewashed pieces to accent the space.

- Add accents of light natural ingredients.

- Be sure to add a lot of subtle patterns and textures to add interest.

COLOR MENU

Ceiling
AquaPearl, Cloud White 967

Walls
AquaPearl, Cloud White 967
washed with Bachelor Blue 1629
and Danish Pewter 973
Norwegian Wood R-9999

Crown accent
AquaPearl, Nordic Gray R-9992
Cloud White 967

STYLE A LA CARTE

Furniture and accessories courtesy of:
Cabinet handles, towel bar, UMBRA/
Vases, white bowl, tissue box, white
trash can, candlesticks, ELTE CARPETS
& HOME/Chair, DE BOER'S.

PAINT TECHNIQUE:

SCANDINAVIAN "LIME" WASH
AND STENCIL
Add a soft and subtly textured look with a
vertical wash and decorative stencil. It will
add height and depth to any room.

INGREDIENTS

3 lint-free rags (1 for each color)

Painter's tape (delicate)

Level

Bucket of water (to wet rags)

Tape measure

Mylar

Utility knife

Stencil design

Paintbrush

Gloves

PAINT

Base coat
AquaPearl, Cloud White 967

First wash coat
AquaPearl, Bachelor Blue 1629

Second wash coat
1 part AquaPearl, Danish Pewter 973
to 1 part water

Finish wash
1 part AquaPearl, Cloud White 967
to 1 part water (optional)

Stencil color
AquaPearl, Cloud White 967
Norwegian Wood R-9999

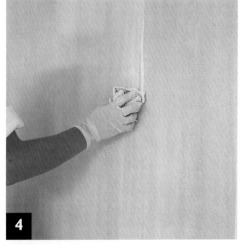

PREPARATION

1. Apply base coat and allow it to dry.

2. Dip rag in water so it is damp. Dip rag into first wash coat of color 1629 and

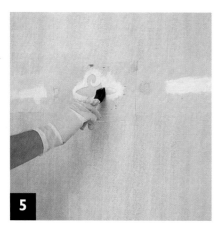

5

apply to the wall in a vertical direction from ceiling to floor. Allow streaks to appear.

3. Continue the first color all the way around the room in the same manner, using a wet rag each time to apply more paint to the wall. Use a brush to get into the corners or difficult areas. Allow first color to dry.

4. Repeat the same process with the second wash coat 973, then the finish wash 967. Allow time for the paint to dry between colors.

5. Tape out location of stencil lines and cut out stencil design from Mylar. Apply paint 967 and R-9999 over the stencil with the brush and allow it to dry.

6. Add a final wash coat in the same manner using 967, if desired, to lighten the look of the walls and stencil.

> "Neutral colors in the manufacturing world include white, black, beige, almond, taupe, gray and silver. The benefit of choosing colors like these is that they tend to blend with most colors and do not date as quickly."

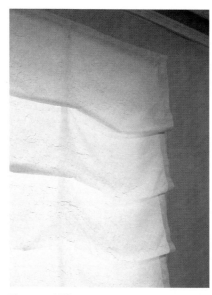

The waterfall Roman blind allows for diffused light, with its semi-sheer fabric. Although linear in design, its loose folds add softness to the angularity of the bathroom.

WINDOW DRESSING:

WATERFALL ROMAN BLIND
(Size: 50 inches x 50 inches)

INGREDIENTS
Fabric:

• 4 meters Elyse, color Rice Paper

10½ meters ring tape

50 inches soft-sided Velcro

50-inch balloon track with components

50-inch weight bar

PREPARATION

1. Measure the fabric to the width of the window plus 4 inches for side hems, and 1½ times the length of the window plus 20 inches. Turn, press and stitch a double 1-inch hem down each side edge. Turn and press a double 1½-inch hem along the bottom edge.

2. Working up the side edge, measure and mark every 12 inches. Mark across the bottom edge every 8 inches. Using these marks as a guide, mark a grid over the back of the blind, keeping the lines straight in each direction. Working with the ring tape, run strips down each vertical row of marks. Tack with a pin, 1 ring at

each mark. The rings are spaced every 8 inches apart; the spacing on the fabric is every 12 inches. Tack each ring through both the tape and the fabric. Clip the ends of the tape at the bottom so that they tuck inside the bottom hem and cut the top ends to be in line with the top of the blind. Continue for each vertical row.

3. Tuck all the ends of the tape inside the bottom hem and stitch. Stitch the soft-sided Velcro along the top edge of the blind. Trim excess and turn to the back and stitch flat. Insert the weight bar and string the blind and attach to the track. Mount as for a normal Roman blind.

Good-taste tip
GRAY EXPECTATIONS
To create a more subdued or sophisticated color tone, select a color that is more gray-based or toned with black. This helps to lower the brightness of the color, so that it feels more subtle but doesn't lack depth.

Colored accents add warmth to this cool environment. A modern chair in natural materials is both functional and decorative.
Both the window covering and shower curtain are made from the same lightly textured fabric to tie the room together.

Bold colors are applied to each of the four walls to add punch to a child's room. Investment pieces, such as furniture and fabrics, are kept neutral, so that only the painted surfaces will need updating as the child grows. Note how the wall colors are pulled into the artwork.

BOLD BASICS: CHILD'S BEDROOM

Add punch to a room with paint – while being practical at the same time! Apply color only to the surfaces that are easily changed, while retaining the natural or neutral colors of more permanent items.

TRIADIC COLOR SCHEME WITH NEUTRALS

SECRET INGREDIENTS

- Pass on primary colors and pick other colors instead.
- Select strong wall colors that balance each other.
- Stick to graphic shapes.
- Allow your kids to select wall colors.

COLOR MENU

Walls
AquaPearl, Jester R-9975
Nightfall R-9978
Prairie Lily R-9927
Sea Grass R-9937

Trim and doors
AquaPearl, Turret R-9993

Ceiling
Wall Satin, Cloud White 967

STYLE A LA CARTE

Furniture and accessories courtesy of:
Table and chairs, easel, wood blocks on table, single bed, side table/ storage box, laundry bag, closet handles, IKEA/Bedding, REVELLE HOME FASHIONS.

PAINT TECHNIQUE:

PAINTED FILING CABINET

This is an easy way to turn an old metal filing cabinet into a unique, useful and colorful storage chest.

INGREDIENTS

6 high-foam rollers and 3-inch trays
Sandpaper, 220-grit
Cloth
Bucket of water
Gloves
Dust mask
2½-inch paintbrush (nylon)

PAINT

Primer
Fresh Start Super Adherent Latex Primer

Drawer colors
AquaPearl, Jester R-9975
Nightfall R-9978
Prairie Lily R-9927
Sea Grass R-9937

Cabinet color
AquaPearl, Turret R-9993
Stays Clear high-gloss latex urethane

Optional:
For alkyd paint, switch to Satin Impervo or Metal Finishes (Regal Signature colors are not available in alkyd paint).

PREPARATION

1. In a well-ventilated area, sand the filing cabinet to remove the gloss from the finish. This is important so that the

An old filing cabinet was refurbished for a colorful child's storage unit. Each drawer picks up one of the wall colors, while the body of the cabinet is painted the same color as the room's trim. Be sure to prime the cabinet first with Fresh Start before applying latex paint. For extra durability, use Satin Impervo instead.

primer will adhere properly.

2. Coat all surfaces with the primer, using a foam roller and brush. Allow it to dry overnight. (Primer not required if using Metal Finishes products.)

3. Apply the body color of the cabinet with a foam roller and allow it to dry.

4. Apply each of the 4 drawer colors and allow each to dry. All surfaces will require at least 2 coats of paint. (For more protection, clear-coat with Stays Clear high-gloss latex urethane.)

PAINT TECHNIQUE:

EVERY-WHICH-WAY WALLS

This paint method uses four of your favorite colors on the walls of one room. It may be a little daring for some people, but it certainly inspires fun.

INGREDIENTS

9½-inch paint cage

4 (9½-inch) roller sleeves

2-inch painter's tape (delicate)

Tape measure

Level

4 (12-inch × 12-inch) artist's stretcher frames and canvas to fit

Staple gun

PAINT

Walls

AquaPearl, Jester R-9975
Nightfall R-9978
Sea Grass R-9937
Prairie Lily R-9927

Trim

AquaPearl, Turret R-9993

Accent

AquaPearl, Cloud White 967

PREPARATION

1. Apply the paint colors to the 4 walls of the room, 1 color per wall. Wrap the color up onto the ceiling until it meets the stipple. (A 4-inch flat area was left unstippled around the room.) Each color will be mitered into the corner of the ceiling, using low-tack painter's tape to separate each color as paint is applied.

2. In the center of each wall, tape out a 24-inch × 24-inch square and paint with R-9993. Allow it to dry.

3. All around the square, tape out a 1-inch band and paint with 967.

4. In each of the corners of the square, paint 1-inch squares in 1 of the other wall colors. Allow to dry completely.

5. In the center of each square, hang your favorite art or let your child paint his own picture, using the colors of paint in the room.

6. Staple the canvas artwork to the back of the stretcher frame, so the wood frame enhances the picture.

Traditional closet-door handles are replaced with brightly colored plastic drawer pulls. Here, six pulls at a variety of heights make it easy for little hands to open the doors.

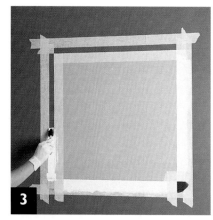

Unique children's artwork is created by stapling a canvas sheet to a wood stretcher frame hung on a taupe painted square. It is set off with a white border and four colored corners.

Roman blinds that fit inside the window frame are made in a taupe fabric to match the room's trim. The window is neutralized and the bold colors of the room stand out.

WINDOW DRESSING:

TAILORED ROMAN BLIND WITH OVERLAY DETAIL

(Size: 27 inches x 50 inches)

INGREDIENTS

Fabric:

- 2.5 meters Alicia, color Mink
- 2.25 meters blackout lining

27-inch long soft-sided Velcro

Plastic rings

27-inch weight bar

Track with components

Piping

PREPARATION

1. Measure the width of the window and add 4 inches. Measure the length and add 20 inches. Cut 1 layer of fabric 31 inches x 70 inches. Cut 1 layer of blackout lining to 29 inches x 65 inches. For the overlay, cut a triangle from the main fabric, 29 inches across the top and 30 inches from the center top to the longest point. Cut 1 layer of blackout lining to the same dimensions. Place a length of covered piping along each of the sides of the triangle on the main fabric. Place the blackout lining

right-sides together on the piped triangle and stitch along the 2 sides. Clip across the point and trim the seams. Flip right-sides out and press flat. Stitch across the top edge.

2. On main fabric, turn and press a double 1-inch seam down each side. Insert the lining under the side folds, working with wrong sides together. Stitch down each side. Turn and press the bottom edge to the back 1 inch and then turn and press back 4 inches. Stitch along the top fold through all layers. Stitch a second line 1-inch below the first to form the pocket for the weight bar.

3. Mark a grid on the back of the blind, beginning above the weight-bar pocket and at evenly spaced intervals, approximately every 8 inches apart in each direction. Sew a plastic ring at each mark. Place the overlay right-side up on the front of the blind, aligning the top edge. Stitch. Place the soft-sided Velcro along the top front of the blind and stitch along the bottom edge of the Velcro. Trim away the excess fabric and fold the Velcro to the back. Stitch along the bottom edge of the Velcro through the blind layer only. Insert the weight bar and string the blind.

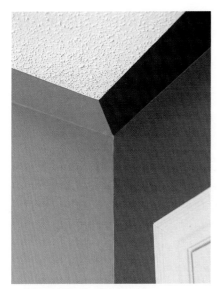

Bold wall colors wrap up onto the flat area of the ceiling to frame its stippled center. The mitered corners frame the ceiling visually and help to raise the height of the ceiling.

Oversize canvas pillows are decorated with painted handprints in the colors of the walls.

A white ceiling fixture is given pizzazz with the addition of four bright colors painted on the ceiling above. The white stipple is scraped away, so that color can be applied easily.

Faux painted bead-board wainscoting instantly creates the ambience of an old beach cottage. Bright starfish accents add pizzazz to the subdued colors of this weathered style. Wood shelves are given the same finish as the faux bead board. The fabric tank cover masks the harsh white of the tank, while integrating the colors of the room. The assorted unmatched bath towels hung on the wall add to the feeling of a comfortable, old beach house.

BEACH HOUSE: POWDER ROOM

This look is sun-drenched, casual, relaxed and easy. It is a wonderful light style that is harmonious with water, washed materials and sun-drenched surfaces. Add beach trinkets to the design for some fun and color – after all, life's a beach!

ANALOGOUS COLOR SCHEME WITH COMPLEMENTARY ACCENTS

- Add lots of weathered textures to surfaces and materials.
- Choose bright sea, sky and sand colors for walls and floors.
- Accent with shells and classic stainless-steel beach buckets.
- Add some soft and wavy lines within the design.
- Don't forget to add a splash of bright color.
- Accent with pictures of family vacations to beach resorts.

COLOR MENU

Walls
AquaPearl, Marble White 942

Wainscoting
AquaPearl, Deep Cove R-9971
Harbour Breeze R-9956

Starfish
AquaPearl, Malibu R-9917

Ceiling
AquaPearl, Cloud White 967
Harbour Breeze R-9956
Mistral R-9963

STYLE A LA CARTE

Furniture and accessories courtesy of:
Metal buckets on toilet, metal tapered buckets, lantern, mirrors, metal towel hooks, shelves, IKEA/Ceiling beams, KEN BALCER/Toilet-tank cover, MARY DOBSON/Decorative birds and shells, SNEZANA BACANIN.

PAINT TECHNIQUE:

FAUX WEATHERED BEAD BOARD

Stir up a pinch of paint with a dry-brush technique to create the saltwater weathered effect seen on a beach house's wainscoting and trim.

INGREDIENTS

¼-inch painter's tape
2½-inch angled sash brush
4-inch foam roller tray set
Sandpaper, medium-grit

PAINT

Base
AquaPearl, Deep Cove R-9971
Harbour Breeze R-9956

Dry-brush
AquaPearl, Cloud White 967

PREPARATION

1. Paint a base coat of R-9971 from floor to chair-rail height (approximately 32 to 36 inches). Allow it to dry thoroughly.

2. Tape vertical stripes, using ¼-inch tape, from top of baseboard to chair-rail height. Leave approximately 3 inches between stripes.

3. Using a foam roller, lightly roll R-9956 on the wall in a vertical motion, allowing some of the R-9971 to be exposed. Continue this around the room, then allow it to dry.

4. Dip the brush into 967 and remove the excess on a rag. Begin dry-brushing with the white over the R-9956 in a vertical

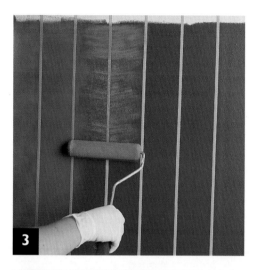

motion. Some areas may appear white, but overall you should be able to see areas with all 3 colors.

5. When dry, remove tape and lightly sand some random areas, again in a vertical manner, to add to the sun-bleached weathered look.

6. Top off the bead board with a wooden chair rail, painted in the same manner as the wainscoting. Repeat the weathered process on trim and doors.

PAINT TECHNIQUE:

STARFISH BORDER

Add a touch of sea life with this textural border motif.

INGREDIENTS

8½-inch × 11-inch piece of fun foam for stencil

Utility knife

Repositioning spray adhesive

Plaster trowel/spackle knife

2-inch painter's tape

Tub of ready-mix drywall compound

Sea sponge

PAINT

Paint

AquaPearl, Marble White 942

Primer

Fresh Start Super Adherent Latex Primer

Starfish

AquaPearl, Malibu R-9917

PREPARATION

1. Cut starfish-shaped stencil out of the easy-to-cut foam with utility knife.

2. Make evenly spaced pencil or chalk markings around the perimeter of the room for easy stencil placement (about 1½ feet apart).

3. Spray adhesive onto stencil and position on wall. Trowel the compound into and onto the stencil, ensuring that the compound fills all corners of the stencil.

4. Lightly texture compound with sea sponge. Remove stencil carefully, leaving a positive impression of the starfish on the wall.

5. Repeat step 3 around the room to create a textured border. When compound is thoroughly dry (time varies according to thickness), prime starfish with Fresh Start primer.

6. Dry-brush R-9917 over starfish to accent the relief pattern.

PAINT TECHNIQUE:

CLOUD CEILING

Painting clouds on the ceiling is a great way to bring the outdoors in.

INGREDIENTS

High-volume low-pressure sprayer (available at home-improvement centers)

Drop sheets

2-foot × 2-foot sample board

Respirator

2-inch painter's tape

PAINT

AquaPearl, Cloud White 967
Harbour Breeze R-9956
Mistral R-9963

PREPARATION

1. Drape all the furniture and flooring in the room with large drop sheets in preparation for spraying. Apply a base coat of 967 to a sample board first. Apply to the ceiling and any other areas where you wish to

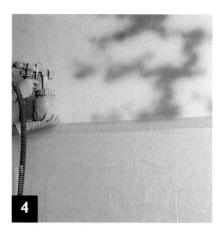

see the cloud technique. Allow to dry for 12 hours.

2. Thin down R-9956 with water, according to the directions on your spray equipment (e.g., 1 part water to 2 parts paint.)

3. Wearing a respirator, test out your spray on the sample board to ensure that you have thinned down the paint adequately and are comfortable using the equipment. Your sprayer should be set to a fine spray. Test out the technique by painting the *blue sky* around the clouds. Try not to paint out too much of the white. It's easier to add more blue later than to remove it.

4. Begin spraying the blue sky, leaving the white base coat exposed in several areas to represent the clouds.

5. Repeat steps 3 and 4 with R-9963 (the slightly darker blue paint) over the first color.

6. If necessary, do a final spray with your 967 base coat color. This should only be necessary if you wish to reveal more cloud areas that have been covered with blue.

NOTE:

If you are not comfortable using spray equipment, look at Benjamin Moore's Paint A Great Impression (page 74) for another easy cloud technique.

"Feel free to rebel against the outside shell of your home. If you live in a modern high-rise condo but dream of living in the Caribbean, you may want to create an entirely different feel on the inside."

The fabric tank cover brings together the key colors of the room. Face cloths are stashed in metal pails for a high-tech take on old-fashioned beach buckets.

Two round mirrors hung at different levels recreate the look of portholes in a ship at sea. A traditional outdoor candle lantern adds a touch of ambient lighting to the room.

"One of the most overlooked surfaces in any room is the ceiling. The ceiling should be an important consideration in the color choices of the room."

Hollow wood beams are installed 12 inches below the nine-foot ceiling to make the painted blue sky above appear more distant.

A faux runner is painted on the stair risers to create warmth and beauty in this Renaissance-inspired foyer. The warm wash on the walls picks up the color of the traditional carpet and bronze and gold decorative accents. Dark stained wood frames the light trim and spindles.

A style that comes from a time gone by, this look captures the aged finishes of the relics we see today. Although this is a look that appears to have aged through time, you can capture its air of elegant decay today.

COMPLEMENTARY COLOR SCHEME WITH NEUTRALS

SECRET INGREDIENTS

- Use deep rich colors on walls, floors and furniture.
- Add Gothic-style touches, such as an arched window or triptych (a 3-panel picture).
- Use touches of gold or silver on furniture and accessories.
- Select rich fabrics, such as tapestries or velvets, for drapery and furniture.
- Add an old chandelier to the space or, even better, a suit of armor – if you can find one!

COLOR MENU

Walls
AquaPearl, Sistine 1103

Wall wash
AquaPearl, Raphael R-9901
Baroque R-9935

Trim
AquaPearl, Fresco R-9957

STYLE A LA CARTE

Furniture and accessories courtesy of:
Chair, rug, lion head, chandelier, candle sconce, table lamp, mirror, light, table, pictures, tapestry, ELTE CARPETS & HOME.

PAINT TECHNIQUE:

VENETIAN WASH

To create a plaster-finish effect and the feeling of the Italian Renaissance, all you need is paint and some old rags.

INGREDIENTS

3 cotton rags
3 buckets
Stir sticks
Gloves

PAINT

Base coat
AquaPearl, Sistine 1103

Wash colors
AquaPearl, Baroque R-9935, Raphael R-9901, each mixed 1 part paint to 1 part water to 1 part AquaGlaze

PREPARATION

1. Apply base coat to walls and allow it to dry.
2. Mix 1 part R-9935 to 1 part AquaGlaze and 1 part water in a bucket. In a second bucket, repeat mixing process, using R-9901.
3. Using a damp rag, dip into bucket of first color and dab off excess on extra paper or cardboard. Apply to wall in a random circular fashion, covering the base color.
4. Complete wall with first color and allow it to dry.
5. Repeat steps 3 and 4 with second color and allow it to dry.
6. To apply wash to corners, use a paintbrush.

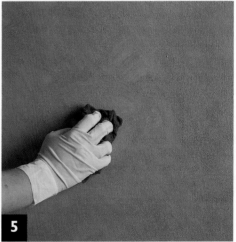

7. In a third bucket, add 1 part glaze, 2 parts water and 1 part base color.
8. Apply to wall with rag in large circles to even out visual texture. Complete wall.

NOTE:

For extra durability in high-traffic areas, roll a coat of Stays Clear low-luster latex urethane on top.

PAINT TECHNIQUE:
STONE BLOCK COLUMNS AND ARCHITECTURAL DETAILS

Re-create the atmosphere of an ancient castle with this technique.

INGREDIENTS

¼-inch painter's tape

Level

Tape measure

Bag of silica sand

3 buckets

Stir sticks

9½-inch roller and tray

2 sea sponges

Artist's brush

PAINT

Paint

AquaVelvet, Florentine Plaster 976
London Fog 1541
Mortar R-9991

Shadow line

AquaVelvet, Overcoat R-9989

PREPARATION

1. Paint a base coat with 976. This will be your grout color. Allow to dry.

2. When base is thoroughly dry, tape off stone block patterns, so that each stone is 12 inches high and 16 inches long.

3. In a bucket, mix 2 cups silica sand into 1 liter base of 976.

4. Roll over the tape lines with 1 coat of paint-and-sand mixture. Allow it to dry.

5. Pour 2 parts of 1541 into a bucket, top with 3 parts water and stir well with a stir stick. In the other bucket, mix the same proportion of water with the R-9991 paint color.

6. Dip first sea sponge into bucket of R-9991 paint mixture and wring out, so that sponge is not dripping. Begin to sponge randomly over surface with thinned-down paint.

7. Repeat step 6 with the 1541 paint mixture.

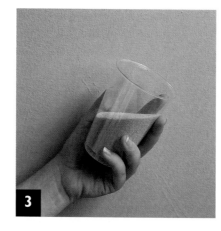

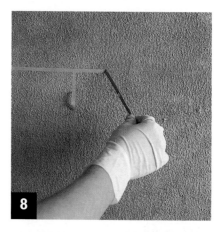

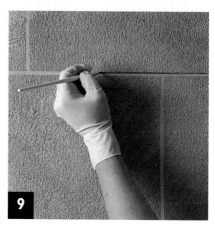

8. Remove tape when sponging is complete and touch up any runs on the grout line with base-coat color.

9. For a more realistic look, use an artist's brush to add a shadow to the top of the grout line with R-9989.

NOTE:

This is a permanent finish.

Good-taste tip
PATIENCE FOR PAINT

Before you rush to a conclusion about the paint color you have applied to the wall, remember that latex paint can take anywhere from 14 to 28 days to fully cure. Only at this point will you really know the true paint color and sheen.

"Since texture is often a subtle element of a material, it is easier to add unique textures within a space without compromising the overall unity."

The upper hallway's bronze-colored washed walls are enhanced by a large traditional tapestry, while the unique hanging fixture adds style and light to the space.

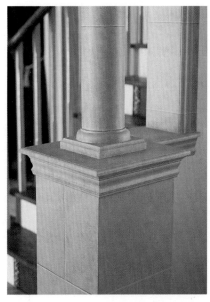

A light sponging technique transforms two plain wood columns into traditional cut stone pillars.

Heavy burgundy curtains replace standard doors to add dramatic flair.

Square-cut spindles are highlighted with a vertical gold accent line along the corner edges.

A Renaissance retreat is created in the upper hallway by adding a built-in wood window bench and rich balloon curtains. The area is defined by two ceiling-mounted drapes with tie-backs.

WINDOW DRESSING:

BALLOON CURTAINS
AND GATHERED PANELS
ON STATIONARY RODS
(Size: 40 inches x 54 inches)

BALLOON CURTAINS

INGREDIENTS
Fabric:

• 5 meters Barcelona, color Mahogany

• 4 meters lining

3 meters shirring loop tape

40-inch-long Velcro track with balloon components and brackets (aluminum balloon track)

½-inch plastic rings

Roman blind cord

PREPARATION

1. Cut 2 widths of fabric to 74 inches Cut the lining to the same dimensions. Join 2 widths of fabric together. Trim the selvage off the 2 outer edges, then turn and press a double 1-inch hem to the back on each. Piece the lining together in the same manner and trim the 2 outer edges to bring the lining width down to the total flat width of the main fabric, once the side hems have been pressed.

2. Aligning the top and bottom ends of the lining and the fabric, insert the cut sides of the lining under the pressed edges of the fabric. Stitch the side hems. At the top end, press the fabric to the back 1 inch. Place the shirring tape along the folded edge and trim the ends of the tape 1 inch longer than the fabric on either end. Turn these ends under and stitch along the top and bottom edges of the tape.

3. Cut 3 widths of fabric 20 inches long and stitch together. Hem across bottom and both ends. Gather down to width of main section and stitch to the bottom. Overcast raw edge. Mark the rings in 8-inch increments up from the top of the gathering. Mark 1 row up the center of each side hem and along the center seam. The remaining rows of rings should be evenly spaced across the width of the fabric, approximately 18 inches apart horizontally (3 rows of rings on each side of the center row for a balloon this size). Stitch rings in place. Gather shirring tape at top.

4. Tie the cord to the bottom ring of each row. The cord should pass through each consecutive ring up to the carrier on the track. Whether the controls are on the right or on the left will determine the direction the cord should travel across the carriers. Repeat this process for each row of rings until all the cords exit at the same side of the balloon. The 2 bottom rings in each row can be tied together, so that the balloon will never be flat from top to bottom, whether up or down.

5. Attach the brackets to the wall and install the track. The cords should be adjusted to the same tension and trimmed to the same length. Tie a knot in the cords at the top when the balloon is down, and braid the cords for a tidy appearance. A cord cleat should be attached to the side of the window frame on the operating side to tie off the balloon at the desired length.

GATHERED SIDE PANELS
(Size: 96-inch length)

INGREDIENTS
Fabric:

• 5.75 meters Spoleto, color Spice (allow extra fabric for matching pattern)

• 6 meters lining (optional)

4 drapery weights

1 pair stationary rods

PREPARATION

1. For each panel, cut the fabric to 108 inches. Remove the selvage from the sides of the fabric. Turn, press and stitch a double 4-inch hem at the bottom. Turn and press a double 1-inch hem at the side edges.

2. Measure the lining to a finished length of 101 inches. Trim the sides of the lining so they are equal with the pressed side edges of the fabric. Turn, press and stitch a double 3-inch hem. With wrong-sides together, place the lining side edges under the pressed edges of the fabric. The bottom edge of the lining should be 1 inch above the bottom edge of the main fabric in a parallel line. Stitch the side hems of the panels. Tack a drapery weight inside the bottom corners of each panel.

3. Turn and press 1 inch back along the top edge of the panel and turn again 3 inches. Stitch a line across the top of the panel 1 inch down from the top fold. Stitch a second line along the bottom folded edge of the same section and gather onto rods.

Renaissance-inspired elements, such as the velvet chair, dark wood mirror and elegant lamp, bring this foyer to life.
The plaster lion's head in the faux-block alcove adds a stately touch.

"Public space is the space that guests,
neighbors, friends, family and visitors will see
when they come to your home."

A comfortable oatmeal-colored sofa and chair add tailored flair to this living area. The chocolate-brown floor is brightened by the light textured fabric of the softly sculpted drapery. Rich wood furniture adds warmth and a touch of tradition to this room.

It is possible to add depth and interest to a space with very little color. Just ensure that you have a good mix of textures and different values of your neutral tones. This look has clean lines and is free of ornamentation, but is rich with subtle pattern, sheen and texture.

ANALOGOUS COLOR SCHEME

- Keep lines and forms simple.
- Select a fairly mono-chromatic color scheme.
- Use matte textured and natural materials.
- Try not to use any pure whites or pure blacks. Choose dark browns or light creams instead.

COLOR MENU

Wall base
AquaPearl, Fresco 957

Wall decorative color
AquaPearl, Sistine 1103

Ceiling
Wall Satin, Richmond Gray HC96

Floor stain
Danish Walnut

Baseboards
AquaPearl, Providence Olive HC98

Trim
AquaPearl, Fresco 957

Stencil accent
AquaPearl, Bullrush R-9932

Crown molding
AqualPearl, White Down 970

STYLE A LA CARTE

Furniture and accessories courtesy of: Table lamps, sisal carpet, decorative bowl, IKEA/Floor lamp, framed photographs, armchair, sofa and chair, pillows on sofa, DE BOER'S/Chests, area carpet, dining table and chairs, chandelier, ELTE CARPETS & HOME/Pictures above chest, NANCY LOCKHART/Wine rack, BRAD JENSEN/End table, topiary trees, MARY DOBSON/Pictures over sofa, SHARON GRECH/Violin, JENNIFER WALTERS.

PAINT TECHNIQUE:

BRUSHED LINEN

This is an easy way to create soft natural texture on any wall, simply by using a scrub brush.

INGREDIENTS

Plastic-bristle scrub brush

2-inch painter's tape (delicate)

9½-inch roller and tray

Bucket

Stir stick

Gloves

Utility knife

Tape measure

Level

PAINT

Base coat
AquaPearl, Fresco 957

Decorative coat
1 part AquaPearl, Sistine 1103 to 10 parts AquaGlaze

PREPARATION

1. Apply base coat and allow to dry.
2. Mix glaze with paint in a bucket. The mixture is 10 parts glaze to 1 part paint.
3. Roll glaze on to wall in 4- to 5-foot sections from baseboard to ceiling.
4. Using the bristle brush, randomly remove the glaze by brushing the wall in short sweeping motions. Continue this until the whole area is completed, except for the wet edge.

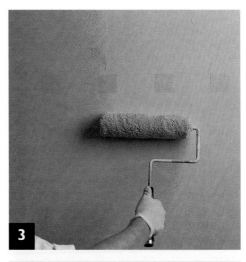

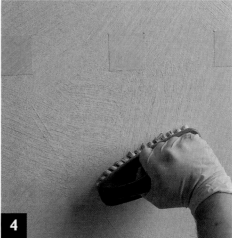

5. Roll out another section of glaze and continue the technique. Finish walls in this manner and allow to dry.

NOTE:

To get into corners, use the edge of the brush or a regular paintbrush to create the look of texture with the glaze.

OPTIONAL:

To add square detail at chair-rail height:

1. Apply tape at 34 inches above the floor. Make sure the line is level.

2. Mark the tape at 2-inch and then 4-inch and then 2-inch increments.

3. Using a utility knife cut vertically along these markings and remove the 4-inch sections, leaving only the 2-inch squares.

4. Roll glaze over top of these taped squares and proceed with technique. Once paint is dry, remove tape squares to reveal the base color below.

Two-inch squares run around the room to create a soft chair rail, without breaking up the wall surface. Natural accessories, such as the rope-wrapped light fixture, add to the room's simple scheme.

"To make your public spaces flow from one area to the next in a pleasing manner, link them visually by choosing colors that are part of one scheme."

Good-taste tip
BIG-TICKET ITEMS
When selecting colors for a room, pick paint colors to match the most expensive items in the room or the ones you intend to keep. This includes the sofa, area rugs and window coverings. This way, your color choice can't be wrong.

A classic wood dining table and a natural sisal rug fit this room wonderfully.
Uplighting from the Frank Lloyd Wright-inspired lamp adds a warm glow to the soft yellow-green ceiling.

Traditional drapery panels are given grace and style with the addition of knotted side columns, which also create the illusion of height.

WINDOW DRESSING:

GATHERED PANELS WITH
KNOTTED OVERPANELS
(Size: 96 inches)

INGREDIENTS

Fabric:

- 10 meters Illusion, color Corn Husk

2 meters Velcro shirring tape

1.4 meters aluminium tracking with hook tape surface

Drapery weights

PREPARATION

1. Measure and cut 2 widths of fabric to 105 inches. Trim away the selvage at each side. Turn, press and stitch a double 4-inch hem at the bottom edge. Turn, press and stitch a double 1-inch hem along each side. Tack drapery weights inside each bottom corner. Repeat for the second panel. Mark the first as the right panel and the second as the left.

2. Cut remaining width to 135 inches. The remaining length of fabric will form the knotted over-panel. Divide and cut the length of fabric in half from top to bottom. Remove the selvage from the edges of the fabric. Turn, press and stitch a double 1-inch hem along the bottom edge and each side.

3. Working first with the right panel, place the hemmed overpanel right-side up on top of the right side of the main panel. Align the top edges and the right hemmed edges. Baste across the edge 1 inch from the top, through all layers. Press the top edge to the back 1 inch. Place the shirring tape across the back, overlapping the cut edge at the bottom. Trim the ends of the tape 1 inch longer than the panel on each end and tuck the ends under. Stitch along both the top and bottom edges of the tape through all layers. Repeat for the left panel, aligning the left edges.

4. Gather the shirring tape down to 20 inches to 24 inches in width. Cut the tracking to the same width and install. Fix the panels to the tracking. Tie 1 knot in the overpanel down one-third from the top and another one-third from the bottom.

Good-taste tip

SIZING UP THE LOOK

To make a room appear larger, select colors with minimal contrast. To make a room appear smaller, choose a variety of contrasting colors. It is contrast, not necessarily color, that makes a room appear smaller.

"If you have a wood floor in walnut brown, your wall and textile colors should be chosen to complement this element."

Here, wide door trim separating the living room from the dining room is transformed into an elegant design element. The painted arts and crafts-inspired detail captures the feeling of the space through both its design and deep rich colors. Natural-color stained floor squares create a visual break between the two rooms and add interest at the same time.

Bright greens and yellows create an inviting garden-inspired work space. Sunflower-fabric window coverings and cream shutters make the window a focal point. The painted paneling and shelf add texture and an outdoor feel. The work table is created from two painted sawhorses and a sheet of sandblasted glass, so that light from the window can filter through.

A clean but comfortable style, this look capitalizes on the natural beauty of greenery within the home. Touches of color are evident in the florals, but the palette is a fresh collection of shades from nature. Forms are elementary, while the style is practical – with the earthy feel of a country potting shed.

ANALOGOUS COLOR SCHEME

SECRET INGREDIENTS

- Keep colors and textures clean and fresh.
- Add floral patterns, but keep them light.
- Capture as much sunlight within the space as possible.
- Accessorize with silver garden tools and pots.

COLOR MENU

Ceiling
Wall Satin, Solarium R-9920

Trim base
AquaPearl, Topiary R-9944

Top coat
AquaPearl, Mossibility R-9947

Walls
AquaPearl, Kittery Point Green HC119, glazed with Mossibility R-9947

STYLE A LA CARTE

Furniture and accessories courtesy of: Glass desktop, framed wall boxes, table lamp, adjustable trestles, desk chair, metal hooks, folding chairs, shelves on screen, storage units with screen, IKEA/Sisal carpet, ELTE CARPETS & HOME/Shutters, SHADE-O-MATIC/Picket fence file box, KEN BALCER/Desk mat, library ladder, JANE LOCKHART.

PAINT TECHNIQUE:
PAINTED PANELING

Bring the outdoors in by painting a fresh new look on that outdated wood paneling and add to it the pictures you love.

INGREDIENTS

T.S.P or M-83

Sandpaper

Wallpaper paste

Wallpaper smoother

2½-inch angled sash brush

Bucket

Stir stick

Color photocopies of botanicals from drapery fabric

Scissors

Rags

Gloves

2 (9½-inch) rollers and trays

High-density foam roller and tray

PAINT

Primer
Fresh Start Super Adherent Latex Primer

Base paint
AquaPearl, Kittery Point Green HC119

Top coat
8 parts AquaGlaze to 1 part AquaPearl, Mossibility R-9947

PREPARATION

1. Wash paneling with soap and water. Allow to dry. Sand completely to de-gloss surface. Wash with T.S.P or M-83, then rinse with clear water to remove any additional gloss. Allow the wall to

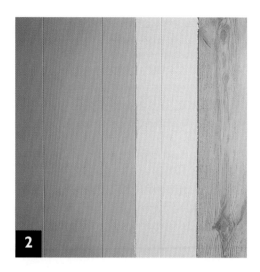

dry. Roll on 1 coat of primer and allow to dry.

2. Roll on 2 coats of base color and allow to dry. Select botanicals from fabric and photocopy desired images. Take each image and tear edges of paper to give a rough edging.

4

3. Apply wallpaper paste to back of each image and place on widest strip of paneling. Smooth paper to surface, using wallpaper smoother, and wipe away excess paste with rag. Be sure to avoid getting glue onto photocopied surface. Allow to dry.

4. Make glaze-and-paint mixture and roll over botanical image. Rag surface to even out rolled glaze.

5. Repeat on each strip where an image has been applied. Allow it to dry.

PAINT TECHNIQUE:
CRACKLE-FINISH SHELVES AND BASEBOARDS

This technique gives a natural weathered look to ordinary trim.

INGREDIENTS
Fish glue (available at Lee Valley Tools, some paint and hardware-supply stores)

2 (1-inch) craft paintbrushes

Large paper plate

PAINT
Primer
Fresh Start Super Adherent Latex Primer

Base coat
AquaPearl, Topiary R-9944

Crackle coat
AquaPearl, Mossibility R-9947

Top coat
Stays Clear low-luster latex urethane

PREPARATION
1. Paint shelves with base coat R-9944. (If shelves are raw wood, prime first with Primer for a smooth surface that can be painted.)

2. Squeeze a substantial amount of glue onto a tray or large paper plate. Wet craft brush, and then dip into glue. (Throw out brush after glue application is finished.)

3. Brush a thin coat of glue onto shelf in a linear fashion. Cover entire surface, but try to avoid thick clumps of glue or overbrushing.

4. Allow glue to become tacky. With a new brush, paint your top coat R-9947 over the glue. As latex paint reacts with the tacky glue, the crackle finish will begin to appear.

5. Wait at least 5 days for glue to cure, then apply 3 coats of urethane for protection.

4

This crackle-finish shelf adds a weathered outdoor feel to an interior room. It's also an ideal spot to display garden artifacts, such as twig balls and miniature chairs.

Good-taste tip
HEADS UP!
Color applied to the ceiling generally appears slightly darker than the same color applied to the wall, because the ceiling receives approximately 30 percent less light than other surfaces in a room. The only time a ceiling color will appear brighter than the chip is if uplighting is directed upon it.

An old screen door becomes a unique wall-mounted shelving unit. Two shelves are added to the face of the door to store and display garden tools and accessories.

Before

Roman blinds with pleated detailing are the color inspiration for the workroom. Here, window boxes are placed indoors, for an outdoor garden feel.

WINDOW DRESSING:

BUTTON-DETAIL BOX-PLEAT BALLOONS

(Size: 30 inches x 67 inches)

INGREDIENTS
Fabric:

- 2 meters Hanover, color Mint
- 2 meters drapery lining

12 self-covered buttons

1 meter soft-sided Velcro

Balloon track and components

Weight bar

Good-taste tip
MELLOW YELLOW

For dark rooms with little light or spaces you want to brighten up, use a yellow or a yellow-based color. Yellows have the highest reflection of light, making a room appear brighter.

PREPARATION

(These instructions are for a large-scale floral stripe.)

1. Cut 1 width of fabric to 80 inches. Remove the selvage from the side edges and turn and press a double 1-inch hem down each side. Cut 1 width of lining to the same length and trim the sides to make it the same width as the pressed width of the main fabric. Place the lining wrong-sides together with the main fabric. Tuck the side edges of the lining under the pressed edges of the main fabric. Machine-stitch the side hems in place. Baste across the top edge to keep the layers in place. Turn, press and stitch a double 1 inch hem along the bottom edge.

2. Working with the flat width of the window and using the narrow stripe of the fabric as a guide, work out the number and size of pleats required to reduce the fabric to the finished width. Centering on each narrow stripe, form a double inverted box pleat and press flat. Depending on the layout of the pattern, you may or may not have single pleats at each side edge. Baste across top.

3. Working on the back of the balloon, mark a line 4 inches from the bottom edge. Cut a length of lining 3½ x 2-inches wider than the finished balloon (32 inches). Turn all the edges to the back 1 inch and press. Place wrong-side down above the placement line. Stitch through all layers at the top and bottom edges.

4. Working on the back, mark the placement of rings every 8 inches up each side edge and up the center of each pleat, beginning at the top of the weight-bar tunnel. Stop within 8 to 12 inches from the top edge. Sew each ring in place. Working on the front of the balloon, tack the box pleats together where each ring is sewn and then sew a button over the tacking. See *Renaissance Revival* balloon instructions on page 58 for finishing.

"Color is the fastest way to create *wow* in any room. A space that has *wow* is a space that has true character and pleases all your senses."

Plain sliding doors reinforce the room's outdoor theme with the use of a stencil cut to look like a wrought-iron gate.

"A private room should be treated as a getaway – something different than the rest of the house and day-to-day living."

For a real garden-shed feel, hang folding wooden chairs at varying heights on the wall. The sunflower motifs are reproductions of the window coverings.

"Difficult rooms are those with fixed items that are expensive or time-consuming to remove. You are best to integrate these items into a scheme and make them a part of it."

Light-colored cabinets, textured yellow walls and mottled beige floor tiles form the perfect backdrop for the brightly colored backsplash, dishes and accessories, all reminiscent of the Mediterranean. Wrought-iron furniture and cabinet knobs add to the mood.

MEDITERRANEAN BREEZE:
KITCHEN/FAMILY ROOM

This look is graphic, clean, bold and simple. Strong colors, such as cool blues and warm reds and yellows, are placed against each other for contrast. Add spice to any space with this citrus-and-cypress Mediterranean styling.

COMPLEMENTARY COLOR SCHEME

- Add the look of tile wherever possible.
- Mix raw metals with old wood furniture.
- Add a few weathered accent pieces.
- Accessorize with terra-cotta pots and olive-oil jars.

COLOR MENU

Ceiling
Wall Satin, Cloud White 967

Trim
AquaPearl, Fresco 957

Base wall
AquaPearl, Semolina 199

Decorative wall colors
AquaPearl, Cork 1117
Semolina 199

Tile colors
AquaVelvet, Terrazzo R-9928
Blue Grotto R-9967
AquaPearl, Cloud White 967
Cilantro R-9948
Mosaic R-9969
Sundried Tomato R-9925
Villa R-9930
El Greco R-9931
Fusilli 216

STYLE A LA CARTE

Furniture and accessories courtesy of: Dining chairs, yellow chair, area carpet, coffee table, ELTE CARPETS & HOME/All kitchen accessories, IKEA/Blender, OSTER/Refrigerator, stove, dishwasher, CAMCO/ Door pulls, UMBRA/Blue sofa and chair, framed photographs, DE BOER'S/ Artwork, HARBOUR GALLERY.

PAINT TECHNIQUE:

TUSCANY TREATMENT

Soften the stark look of kitchen walls by creating a taste of the Mediterranean.

INGREDIENTS

Large sea sponge
2 (2½-inch) angled sash brushes
2 buckets

PAINT

Base coat
AquaPearl, Semolina 199

Decorative coat
1 part AquaPearl, Semolina 199 to 1 part AquaGlaze and 1 part AquaPearl, Cork 1117 to 1 part AquaGlaze

PREPARATION

1. Apply a base coat of 199 and allow to dry over night.
2. In a bucket, combine 1 part AquaGlaze to 1 part 1117. In a second bucket, repeat using 199.
3. Staying within a 3-foot-square area, use a 2½-inch brush to apply the 1117 mixture to the wall, creating an erratic *lightning rod* pattern.
4. While the paint is still wet, use the other brush to dab the 199 mixture around the pattern. Then blend the 2 colors by pouncing with a slightly damp sea sponge. Work quickly, since the colors blend easily while wet.
5. Continue around the space, repeating steps 3 and 4. Work in a vertical fashion, from the top down.

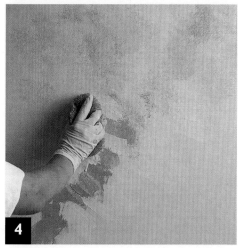

PAINT TECHNIQUE:

FAUX-TILE BACKSPLASH

Although this technique requires a bit of work, the final tiled look can be a wonderful addition to any room.

INGREDIENTS

2½-inch paintbrush

¼-inch painter's tape

10 (3-inch) mini foam rollers and trays

Level

Gloves

PAINT

Base

AquaPearl, Parmesan 190

Tile colors

AquaVelvet, Terrazzo R-9928

Blue Grotto R-9967

AquaPearl, Cloud White 967

Cilantro R-9948

Mosaic R-9969

Sundried Tomato R-9925

Villa R-9930

El Greco R-9931

Fusilli 216

Top coat

Stays Clear high-gloss latex urethane

PREPARATION

1. Paint a base coat of 190 on backsplash area. Allow it to dry overnight before taping.

2. Using painter's tape, apply horizontal lines 4 inches apart along the backsplash. Then tape vertical lines also 4 inches apart to create 4-inch square tiles. Use a level to ensure that tiles are square.

3. Using a foam roller, paint each tile a different color, creating a random pattern. Allow adequate time to dry and then finish with a second coat.

4. Remove tape when all coats are complete and allow it to dry thoroughly.

5. Roll on at least 3 coats of Stays Clear.

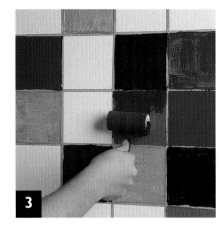

OPTIONAL:

Lightly dip paintbrush into 190. Remove excess by brushing onto a cardboard or paper. Then lightly brush over the tiles to soften edges before applying urethane.

A faux painted backsplash adds a jolt of color to the kitchen, while its aged wash finish creates a feeling of Old World charm. The sun stencil, randomly placed, is inspired by the warmth of the Mediterranean.

"Accent colors add visual energy to a space."

Decorative switch plates add flair to any room. Here, hot-glue designs are applied to a plain plastic switch plate. When dry, the plate is painted to match the wall.

A secondhand baker's rack becomes a perfect storage unit for kitchen accessories. Painted knee-wall shelves provide an attractive, yet functional display area for additional bowls and greenery.

Brightly colored furniture and artwork add punch to the family room. Painted tiles around the fireplace create a focal point and help to link this room to the kitchen. Additional wrought-iron pieces also tie the rooms together.

"Mediterranean blue adds vibrancy and warmth to a terra-cotta scheme."

The strong blue of the sofa and fireplace tiles is carried through to the interior of the cupboards. Doors added to existing shelves allow for hidden storage.

Lively fabric, hung from wrought-iron rods, adds color and texture to the walls.

WINDOW DRESSING:

SCALLOPED TOP PANELS
WITH CORD LOOPS
(Size: 49 inches x 95 inches)

INGREDIENTS

Fabric:

- 5 meters Spoleto, color Multi (allow extra fabric for pattern matching)
- 5 meters drapery lining

3 meters decorative cording

4 drapery weights

Decorative rod

"Live with a new wall color for at least seven days before you decide to change it. It takes time to adjust to a real color change."

PREPARATION

1. For each panel, cut 1 width to 100 inches and cut lining 4 inches shorter and 4 inches narrower. Turn, press and stitch a double 4-inch hem at the bottom edge of the curtain and a double 3-inch hem at the bottom of the lining. Turn and press a double 1-inch hem along each side edge of the main fabric.

2. Working at the top of the main fabric, mark the center point and 1 inch in from each side edge, then 2 more evenly spaced points between the center and each side edge point. Draw a shallow symmetrical dip between each 2 points until you have covered the width of the panel and cut. Duplicate this pattern at the top of the lining layer.

3. Cut the cording into 7 (10-inch) lengths and fold each in half. Place a folded length of cord at each point, placing it on the face of the fabric, with the cut ends of the cord centered on the point. Unfold the side edges of the panel and place the lining right-sides together with the main fabric, aligning the cut top edge. Stitch along the cut edge, 1 inch from the top, stitching straight across each point through the bulk of the cord. Trim the seam allowance and clip into the curve every ½ inch. Do not trim the edges

of the cord. Flip right-side out and press flat. Tuck the side edges of the lining under the pressed side edges of the main fabric and stitch. Insert a drapery weight inside each bottom edge.

Good-taste tip
I'VE SHEEN THE LIGHT!
When you select a paint color from small paint-strip samples, the color is produced in flat paint. If the paint you purchase has more sheen, e.g., a semi-gloss or pearl, the color on the wall will appear darker. The more sheen or gloss you add to your paint, the darker the color will appear.

CHAPTER FOUR

Alfresco

Old-fashioned recipes for exteriors

Many modern homeowners choose white for an exterior color because they believe white is a safe choice and perennially popular. In fact, color is the easiest way to give your home a spectacular exterior.

The early settlers of the eastern seaboard took full advantage of hand-made pigments created from the natural materials and pigments available in the area. While many British homes were made of brick or stone, North Americans used wood sideboard and shingles – all prime areas for paint application. Colors were strong and regionally dictated, depending on the materials available nearby. Painters mixed their own personal set of colors from individual recipes and applied them by hand with large brushes. Whitewashes were made from lime and applied to wood structures to freshen up their look.

By the mid-1800s, dark colors were popular. This was in response to more complex architecture and unique designs made possible by machine lathes, which could create complicated and shapely design ornamentation.

In the Victorian period, every surface was highlighted with texture and color. In response to such ornamentation, North American Colonial Revival styles surfaced, featuring a smoother cleaner style. Lighter colors, such as light blue, gray, yellow and white, became popular.

As the modern movement dawned in the 20th century, residential building became much simpler and color was not a major factor. Materials and texture were important. White, a holdover evolution from the Colonial Revival style, coupled with the modern movement, survived. By the 1950s, everything was white. Stark contrast was added with dark brown, dark green and black trim.

Today, there is a return to color, but some homeowners still hesitate. Our eyes have grown accustomed to white as the exterior color. However, white can actually mask the detailed architecture of a home's face, so that its unique features become difficult to distinguish.

Instead, use color to highlight your home's features and bring out its special character.

EMPHASIZING ARCHITECTURAL FLAVOR

Exterior color choices can create or communicate a particular architectural style. In this case, the color is part of the architectural design of a home's face. This is true whether your home is Victorian, Tudor or even ultramodern.

In each case, colors chosen specifically to represent the

Strong architectural elements, such as the vertical windows and porch columns, are painted white for emphasis in this color scheme. Shutters and garage doors, painted a deeper color than the siding, seem to recede. The focal point is the front door, painted a bright high-gloss red.

Before

period or character of the building further enhance the architectural elements. The contrast and placement of colors are also important. For example, architectural features that are three-dimensional look more dramatic when shades of colors are applied.

The architecture of a particular style of home requires research to ensure that the proper tones have been selected and applied appropriately to illustrate that period. If you have a Victorian home, for instance, you should know that there are very particular guidelines for color choices and placement. Remember: color is one of the most important ways to emphasize the period of your home.

WARMING UP

Many people lack confidence when choosing colors for the inside of their home. At least when these choices are made, they can be corrected, if necessary, in private. Let's face it: most of the neighborhood won't know what colors you chose inside. But the exterior of your home is another story. Any poor color choice will be obvious to all your neighbors – and suddenly everyone will have an opinion.

Choosing a color for the outside of your house may seem daunting, but there are

actually fewer color choices to consider. Your color palette is somewhat predetermined by the building materials – brick, stucco and siding, to name a few.

All **the trimmings**

Your home is one of the largest investments you will ever make, so think of the color choices you select as enhancing your investment. This is not to say that you should not select at least some colors that you really like, but try to choose what will bring out the best character of your home.

For instance, if teal green is your favorite color but your home has yellow-beige brick and a black shingled roof, teal is not the best choice for eaves and trim. Work with the colors the builder chose for the materials used in your home.

Color can actually make a home sell faster and for more money if it enhances the natural character of the structure. Selecting the right colors for your exterior enhances its *curb appeal* for potential buyers.

THE BLENDER APPROACH

During the late 1960s and 1970s, the trend was to apply high-contrast colors to a home.

This complementary combination of colors emphasizes the house's windows and doors. Deep rich colors enhance the light green and taupe siding and give the house a strong presence on its corner lot.

Colors of exteriors shown in photos on page 80:

Plan 1: **Window Trim** – Moorglo Acrylic Latex House & Trim Paint Soft Gloss, 228 **Shutters** – Moorglo Acrylic Latex House & Trim Paint Soft Gloss, 230 **Front Door** – Impervo Alkyd High Gloss Enamel, 1301 **Porch** – Moorglo Acrylic Latex House & Trim Paint Soft Gloss, White
Plan 2: **Window Trim & Porch** – Moorglo Acrylic Latex House & Trim Paint Soft Gloss, Hampshire Gray HC101 **Shutters** – Moorglo Acrylic Latex House & Trim Paint Soft Gloss, Copley Gray HC1499 **Front Door** – Impervo Alkyd High Gloss Enamel, Gloucester Sage HC100
Plan 3: **Window Trim and Porch** – Moorglo Acrylic Latex House & Trim Paint Soft Gloss, Copley Gray HC104 **Shutters** – Moorglo Acrylic Latex House & Trim Paint Soft Gloss, Townsend Harbor Brown HC64 **Front Door** – Impervo Alkyd High Gloss Enamel, Townsend Harbor Brown HC64

For example, white stucco or siding was accompanied by dark brown trim, a black roof and black front door. Although this scheme has drama, it tends to create several different areas of focus. As a result, the front door becomes secondary to other, less important features of the house, such as the eaves and trim. And, just as with interiors, the more contrast added to an object or room, the smaller that item appears. An exterior color scheme is probably one instance where you do want to suggest that your home is larger than it appears. Achieve this by minimizing stark contrast.

Today's choices for exterior colors should be closer to each other in color range. This is not to suggest that the colors should be dull, but rather that they should blend together better to create an overall palette that doesn't have glaring color contrasts. Not only is this the current color direction, it will also bring out the best features of your home, hide some of the less attractive items and make your house appear larger. Accent colors can be selected to highlight certain areas of the house, such as the front door, shutters, plant boxes or decorative trims.

HIGHS AND LOWS

It may seem an odd concept, but the exterior of your house is not flat. It has peaks and valleys, areas that move toward the light and those that recede into shadow. Recognizing that your home has a face should help you to differentiate the assets of the exterior.

Although one area may be more prominent than another, this doesn't necessarily mean that it is worth highlighting. Determining which surfaces are important is the key to making the exterior of your home sing!

MAIN-COURSE COLOR

The main color of your home will look best if it is a mid-tone color. Highlights can be lighter or darker, depending on the style of the home.

In the past, many people chose white as the main body color. Although white does have a crisp fresh feel, it is not as historically relevant as many people think. This look, in fact, was originally achieved with whitewash that, in the end, appeared more light gray than today's sharp and somewhat harsh whites.

In addition, white isn't always the best setting on which to add accent color. Since white is the most reflective and therefore the brightest of colors, it tends to advance and overpower accent colors. And, when paired with strong highlights, high contrast is created, so that the house looks

The color scheme is carried all the way around the house, following the design of the exterior. White porch pickets and columns emphasize the verandah, while the base and capitals of the columns and the handrail are painted to match the shutters and are neutralized. Dormers were also painted to blend into the surfaces around them.

The garage and front door dormers are painted dark green, so that the light trim dominates. Dark verandah columns disappear, allowing the porch pickets and handrail to come forward and draw the eye.

Light shutters and columns stand out in this color combination. Window trim is painted dark green, so that it disappears. The front door dormer is painted dark green to link it to the color of the garage doors. The dark-green front door recedes into the house to give a subtle overall effect.

more like a collection of parts. From a practical point of view, white shows more dirt and grime than other colors, such as muted or gray-toned colors.

Once the body color has been selected, select colors for the eaves, window and door trim.

THE SIDE DISHES: DOORS, TRIM AND MORE

Eaves and downspouts are items that should be colored to blend into the surface against which they are placed. Eaves can either be a color similar to the roof or to the body color. They are not features of the face, so they should be colored to blend into their surroundings.

Window trim, however, can be treated in several ways. If the window frames can be painted, choose a color that is visibly darker or lighter than the body color, but within the same color. They will blend in. Be careful not to select a color that is too strong, so that the window framing doesn't overpower the face of the house.

Keep in mind that your windows are like a woman's eyes: you are applying eyeshadow to the lids. Although you want to enhance this surface, you do not want to make it stand out so much that everything else is lost to the eyeshadow color itself.

GARAGE DOORS

The garage door is one of the most problematic areas for choosing exterior color because it is often the largest feature. Its position, usually at the front, also makes it the most visible. Its location, however, does not make it the most important. In fact, the garage door should be downplayed in the overall color scheme. This is because it will dominate the house and eclipse what should be the most important feature – the front door.

Trim around the garage door itself should match that of the windows, but the door itself is where an additional color choice can be made. This color should not be the same as the front door, as the garage door is

not nearly as important a feature. And because it is so large an area, it is better to help hide its size by blending it into the body color. Essentially, select a color that is either lighter or darker than the overall color, but not the same as the trim.

The appetizers
of a home

Items on the front of the house that are assets are those features that add beauty or charm to the overall character. Assets could include shutters, planters, lattice, gingerbread trim, the front door or any attractive details. Many of these items are small surfaces but deserve maximum highlighting because they are unique and give your home character.

The front door is the most significant of all of these features. Choose a bold accent color that complements the trim and body color. If there is any area that can support a totally different and daring color, this is the place. Do not hesitate to choose a strong color. After all, this is the one area of the house all guests see when visiting your home.

The front porch is extended with the addition of a semi-circular stone step. Its gentle curve softens the angles of the house, while providing a gradual path to the front door. Potted yellow mums add a burst of color.

10 STEPS FOR CHOOSING COLOR

Follow these steps for choosing colors for the exterior of your home:

1. Determine the materials on the house exterior that you intend to keep. This creates a color direction.

2. Get samples of brick, siding, stone and the eaves, if it is pre-colored.

3. Select a range of paint colors that work with the existing exterior materials.

4. Depending on the style of your home, you will need about four different colors – three in similar tones and one bright accent color.

5. Begin by selecting the main color for the surface that you can paint, such as stucco. If the exterior is brick or siding, then begin with this as your main color.

6. Choose a color for the eaves that is similar to the roof color. If it is black, brown or dark gray, choose a color that blends in with the body color to hide drainage pipes and eaves.

7. Choose window and door trim colors. They should contrast with the body color, because they are features to emphasize.

8. For the garage door, choose a color that blends in with the body color. But for variety, choose a color that is slightly lighter or slightly darker.

9. If you have decorative planter boxes, wall lattice or shingles, select a stronger accent color to highlight them.

10. The main accent color should be reserved for the front door. This color can be a lighter or darker shade of the other colors, or something brighter and stronger to draw attention.

1. To make the exterior of your house seem larger, lower the contrast between exterior colors; e.g., don't place dark brown eaves against a white background.

2. Before choosing a color, look at it outside in the sunlight and in the shade.

3. Blend the color of the garage door into the surrounding surfaces by choosing a color similar to the colors around it.

4. Highlight architectural details of a home with a lighter color and downplay negatives with a dark color.

5. If your front door is hidden from view, create a path with potted flowers, accent stones or painted squares on the walkway, patio or porch floor.

6. To add color, select colorful flowers and place them on the front steps or hang them around the door.

7. Focus on important features, such as the porch and front door, by adding polished brass hardware.

8. Dark-colored roofing material fades faster than lighter-colored roofs.

9. Choose a light color for your wood deck or porch floor because it will be less hot to walk on. It will show the dirt less and will not fade as quickly.

10. For a uniform exterior, keep the back of your interior window coverings the same color.

11. A white exterior body color, will take on a slight green tint if it is near a lot of greenery or shrubs. To compensate, select a warm white with a touch of pink in it.

12. Red, burgundy, pink and magenta tend to fade faster in direct sunlight than other colors, so use them in limited amounts.

White shutters are complemented by an ochre stencil, painted in the center of each one. The stencil adds a punch of unexpected color to a monochromatic scheme.

Even plain windows can be decorative with the addition of a hand-cut stencil painted at the base of the window frame.

It is what they look for when driving by. The door's color gives punch to the look of your home. Think of your front door as a pair of lips. It says hello to friends, visitors, neighbors and guests. It's no wonder red is a favorite choice for front doors.

Shutters and window boxes can be the same color as the front door. Remember: if you choose this route, they may end up competing with the door for attention.

Fences, decks and porches

Fences, decks and front porches can be colored to match the trim or body color of the house, depending on the impact you want to create. Even patio stones, stamped concrete and brick pavers can be considered color options. Try to choose a color that blends with the overall color scheme of the house. This will extend the look of your residence, unifying the structure itself and its surrounding features.

Fences and garden sheds or tree houses are an excellent way to continue to integrate exterior colors throughout the property. Wood fences with posts can repeat other colors featured on the house. The more integrated these structures, the more elegant and stylish your home will appear.

Setting the table: your garden

Plants and flowers extend the colors of your home. One of the most important areas to address is the front porch and walkway. Here is a great opportunity to select colors that blend with the front door. For instance, if you choose burgundy as the accent color for the door, then integrate burgundy flowers with some yellow and white flowers. This helps to make the accent color part of the entire look and not just an isolated color on its own.

If the color is used along the entire walkway to the house, it can make the whole house seem larger. If your garden doesn't present you with these opportunities, the

A large wood deck off the kitchen provides a comfortable outdoor dining room on warm summer days. The brightly stained structure gives dimension to an otherwise flat exterior.

Before

An old and tired metal patio set was brought back to life with a coat of black and gold spray paints and new funky fabric on the chair seats and backs.

Decks are a great surface on which to add painted designs in solid stain. The inspiration and colors for this design are taken from the fabric covering the chairs.

STYLE A LA CARTE

Furniture and accessories courtesy of: Chandelier, dishes, IKEA.

An updated table and chairs add ambience to this outdoor dining area. Colors for the deck are inspired by bright fabric used to recover the chair seats and backs. The painted floor design brings the look of an area carpet outdoors.

Painted lattice in square panels acts not only as a wall for hanging exterior decorations, but also as a privacy screen.

Faux painted tile and stone give a plain concrete porch slab a lift. The mottled red and brown tiles blend well with the color of the front door, while leading the eye up to the house entrance.

best way to integrate color and nature is on the front porch. Place urns or pots of flowers flanking the door in colors that blend with the overall house colors.

The pots themselves can also be the accent color, should you choose to plant evergreens or greenery only. Even if the front of your home is plain or doesn't have a lot of outstanding features, selecting colors for the garden that are in keeping with the architectural colors of the house can spice up the look.

Using complementary colors adds drama to an otherwise dull exterior. For example, if your home has yellow brick with a dark-green roof accented with sage green on the eaves and trim and dark plum on the front door, then select purples and lavenders for the dominate garden color. Accent this with white, yellow and fushia. In this case, the purple flowers add life to the yellow brick, because they are complementary colors. When placed together, they intensify each other, adding visual spice to the color combination and, hence, the overall appearance of your home.

Although flowers and plants are beautiful regardless of their colors, it's worthwhile to consider which colors actually enhance the front of your home. Small details can dramatically change the appearance of any home.

SEASONAL TASTES

As the seasons change, particularly in northern climates, the lighting and environment change drastically – from deep snow in winter to lush greenery in summer. This is something you should remember when selecting colors for your home. Although it is unlikely that you will change your exterior colors every winter and summer, it is nice to incorporate the season's colors into your home's face.

Seasonal accents can be created with colored accessories. For instance, in the summer, dress up your front door with a large wreath, using lush strong colors that directly complement the colors of the house. In the autumn, change this wreath to one that incorporates red and gold, or natural materials mixed with accents that complement your home's colors.

Christmas lights are another wonderful accent to any home, so consider the color of the lights you choose. Today, white is the most popular choice and adds a classic touch to even a modern home. But carefully chosen colors and certain color combinations can make a home look that much richer. For instance, blues and greens are lovely and add regal flair, as does the combination of white and purple.

If you want to add a touch of color, wrap lights around potted miniature evergreens and place them on either side of the door. They are easy to install and remove — and the hint of color will complement the front door color as well. It is this attention to detail that creates an interesting color scheme and enriches the appearance and perceived value of your home.

DRESSING IT UP

Although paint is applied to exteriors primarily to give color, it can also be used to create natural and decorative surfaces. Faux finishes have been popular indoors for years, but they are also useful on exteriors. Newly purchased items, such as urns or planting pots, can be made to look like metal with the right paint and special effects. Eaves or metal roofs can be painted for a verdigris effect. Concrete is available in a variety of colored pigments and can be stamped with a pattern so that it resembles granite or terra-cotta tiles.

Windows and doors can be created on flat walls simply by adding a decorative mural or trompe l'oeil. Every type of image can be created on the exterior of your home, as long as the proper paint is used. This is far more critical on your exterior than interior, because the exterior is exposed to harsh elements.

Plastic black urns were aged by first spraying them with gold paint and then applying a brown glaze on top. This is a wonderful way to take an inexpensive plastic object and give it some style and finesse.

The colors of the natural materials and landscaping complement the warm paint colors selected for the exterior of the house. Yellow mums add a bright accent.

A curving natural-stone walkway flows from the driveway up to the verandah. The terra-cotta crushed-stone driveway adds color and depth to the burgundy doors.

Planting beds follow the line of the verandah, culminating in a circular-shaped bed at the corner of the house that softens the angles of the architecture.

Glos**sary**

Although you may feel fairly comfortable with the lyrical names of the colors you select, you should familiarize yourself with the technical lingo that is used by the experts. After all, color is visual and therefore hard to describe. Using the right language can help to eliminate some colorful confusion.

ANALOGOUS COLORS These are three colors found side by side on the color wheel. They often blend well together.

CHROMA Another word for color.

COMPLEMENTARY COLOR This term describes any color opposite another on the color wheel. When complementary colors are placed side by side, they intensify the other, making them appear brighter and stronger.

HUE This describes a color family, such as red or blue.

INTENSITY This term describes the amount of chroma in a particular color. It also refers to the brightness of a color, which is determined by the amount of gray in it.

LAMP This is used to describe the bulb in the light fixture in your house. There are a variety of lamps, including the one we are most familiar with: the regular incandescent light bulb.

LIGHT Although most of us think that a light is something we turn on and off every day, *light* is the true architectural term to describe a window. Hence the term, *skylight*.

PEARLESSENCE This describes a color that has a shimmering or metallic sheen to it when held in the light. This sheen can be applied over top of flat colors.

SHADE This is color that has had black added to it.

SHEEN This is used to describe the relative shine of a color and can be measured from 0 to 100. A flat sheen is in the lower ranges, while semi-glosses and high-glosses are in the 70 to 100 range.

TINT This term refers to the addition of white to a color.

TONE This term describes the original color before black or white has been added to it.

TRIADIC COLORS Three colors on the 12-color color wheel that are equal distance apart (e.g., red, blue and yellow).

VALUE This term refers to the relative lightness or darkness of a color.

Sources

BALMER STUDIOS
271 Yorkland Blvd.
North York, Ont.
M2J 1S5
Tel: 416/491-6425

CAMCO INC.
(Makers of GE and GE
Profile Appliances)
175 Longwood Rd. S.
Hamilton, Ont.
L9N 3Y5
Tel: 905/521-3107

CHARLENE ERICCSSON
Tel: 416/534-7898

DE BOER'S
275 Drumlin Circle
Concord, Ont.
L4K 3E4
Tel: 905/669-9455

ELTE CARPETS & HOME
80 Ronald Ave.
Toronto, Ont.
M6E 5A2
Tel: 416/785-7885

HARBOUR GALLERY
1697 Lakeshore Rd. W.
Clarkson, Ont.
L5J 1J4
Tel: 905/822-5495

IKEA
1065 Plains Rd. E.
Burlington, Ont.
L7T 4K1
Tel: 905/637-9440

JENSEN INTERIORS
1015 Johnson's Lane,
Suite 5
Mississauga, Ont.
L5J 2P6
Tel: 905/403-8444

PRIDE OF PARIS
(Division of Caya
Fabrics)
130 Weber St. W.
Kitchener, Ont.
N2H 4A2
Tel: 1-800-265-0762

PUTTI FINE
FURNISHINGS
1104 Yonge St.
Toronto, Ont.
M4W 2L6
Tel: 416/972-7652

REEVES FLORIST AND
NURSERY
8700 Islington Ave. N.
Woodbridge, Ont.
L4L 1X5
Tel: 905/851-2275

REVELLE HOME
FASHIONS
530 Adelaide St. W.
Toronto, Ont.
M5V 1T5
Tel: 416/703-4533

S&P PAINTING &
DECOR
1511 Otonabee Dr.
Pickering, Ont.
L1V 6T4
Tel: 416/501-2580

SANDI
CONSTRUCTION
Ken Balcer
Tel: 905/338-7891

SHADE-O-MATIC
660 Oakdale Road
Toronto, Ont.
M3N 1W6
Tel: 416/742-1524

SOFA SO GOOD
1769 Britannia Rd. E.
Malton, Ont.
L4W 4E2
Tel: 905/565-0194

SUNBEAM
CORPORATION
(CANADA) LTD.
5975 Flabourne St.
Mississauga, Ont.
L5R 3V8
Tel: 905/501-0090

TAPE SPECIALTIES LTD.
615 Bowes Rd.
Thornhill, Ont.
L4K 2G5
Tel: 905/669-4881

UMBRA LTD.
2358 Midland Ave.
Toronto, Ont.
M1S 1P8
Tel: 416/299-0088

Index

Home **Sweet** Home

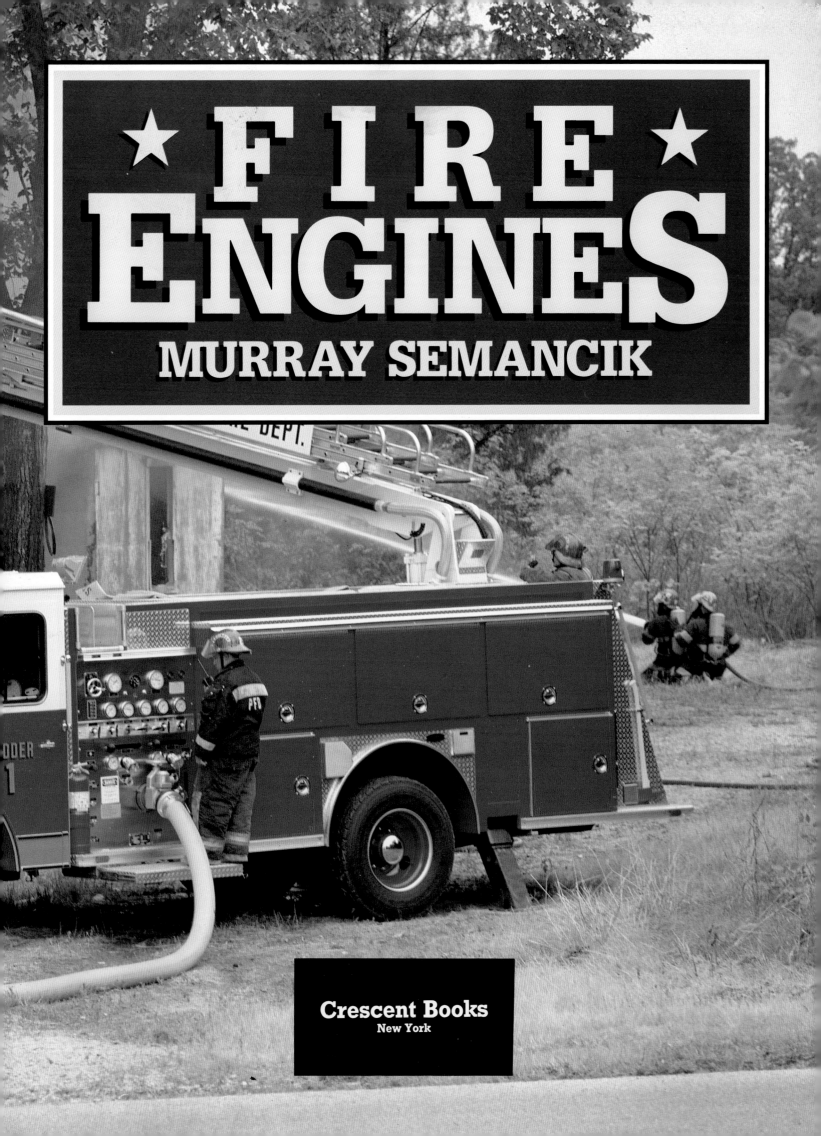

★ FIRE ★
ENGINES
MURRAY SEMANCIK

Crescent Books
New York

4

This 1992 edition published by Crescent
Books,
distributed by Outlet Book Company, Inc.,
a Random House Company,
225 Park Avenue South,
New York, NY 10003.

Produced by
Brompton Books Corporation
15 Sherwood Place,
Greenwich, CT 06830

ISBN 0-517-06701-3

8 7 6 5 4 3 2 1

Printed and bound in Hong Kong

Acknowledgements
The author and publisher express their
thanks to all the manufacturers who
provided material for this book. The author
also wishes to thank John Creighton for
reviewing the manuscript.

All photos appear through the courtesy of
the respective manufacturers with the
following exceptions:
Cigna Museum and Art Collection: 6, 7
John Creighton: 32-33 (bottom)
Ruth DeJauregui: 8, 9 (top), 10 (bottom), 12
   (bottom), 19 (both), 48, 49 (top), 68-69
Fairfield Department of Public Safety, Fire
   Department: 9
Florida Department of Commerce, Division
   of Tourism: 16
J&J Kidd: 10 (top), 11 (bottom), 12 (top)
Bill Yenne: 15 (bottom), 17, 18

Page 1: **A 1990 Sutphen Stainless Steel
Extended Cab Rescue pumper.**

Pages 2-3: **This Emergency One 50 Foot
Teleboom serves the Princeton Volunteer
Fire Department in Kentucky.**

Below: **The Gloucestershire Fire & Rescue Service depends on an Angloco
Aerial equipped with Bronto 28-2T1 Skylift on a Leyland DAF 2500 Chassis.**

CONTENTS

INTRODUCTION

A Brief History of Firefighting Apparatus

The piercing sound of a siren shatters the quiet of the afternoon, and all heads turn to look as a bright red fire engine, decked out in shiny chrome, races down the street, answering the call of a first-due alarm. Since the days of hand pumpers, the clanging of the bells and the wail of the siren has never failed to set the heart racing. The handsome firefighting rigs of today represent the proud heritage of men and machine working together to protect us from one of the most destructive elements known to mankind—fire.

Richard Newsham is generally credited with inventing the first successful fire engine about 1720. A button maker in London's garment district, Newsham simply attached wheels to a water pump and called it a fire engine. His idea wasn't especially brilliant; it wasn't even original, but Newsham's device had something that previous inventors lacked—the support of King George I of England.

Ironically, George I was interested more in watering the royal gardens with the new contraption than he was in its firefighting capabilities, but that didn't stop Newsham from proclaiming that his engine was the choice of royalty.

Newsham's hand-drawn pumpers put out between 70 and 170 gpm—gallons per minute (265-644 l/m—liters per minute) of water, roughly the equivalent of a garden hose, but the stream of water was steady as long as volunteers manned the pump handles. These early pumpers were a definite improvement over the bucket brigade, and word of this wonderful invention soon spread to the American colonies. The city of Philadelphia purchased one Newsham, and New York City soon followed with an order for two. Four days after the pumps arrived in New York, they were put to the test when a house went up in flames. The Newshams failed to extinguish the fire, but

Left: **With its front and back-mounted handles, Richard Mason's 1792 hand pumper was an early improvement over Newsham's pumper.**

Right: **The Pioneer—an 1875 Reaney and Neafie steamer—is today part of the CIGNA Museum and Art Collection.**

New Yorkers nevertheless remained enthusiastic about their purchase.

Outside of New York, however, few communities could afford a Newsham, so volunteer firefighters began crafting their own pumps, often improving the basic design. Richard Mason, a Philadelphia carpenter and member of the Northern Liberty Engine Company, built a pumper with the handles mounted in the front and back rather than on the sides like the Newsham. This modification enabled the volunteers to add water to the tank without getting in the way of the firefighters manning the handles.

Eventually hand-operated pumpers were replaced by horse-drawn, steam-operated pumpers. In 1829, George Braithwaite of London built the first steam-powered fire engine, and it was readily embraced by Londoners. In the United States, however, the transition from hand pumps to steam-operated ones was much slower in coming, not until just before the Civil War. By the 1820s and 1830s, hand-drawn pumpers had grown quite large—some required 50 men to operate—and the volunteers felt confident using them. Horse-drawn, steam-operated

pumpers would require fewer men—and therein lay the problem. The heroes of song and story, volunteer fire companies had achieved a high level of social and political status and they were loathe to relinquish their power.

This was the era of New York's 'Boss' Tweed, himself a captain of a volunteer company, and the corrupt Tammany Hall political machine, which gained its early momentum from the large volunteer force. The ranks of the volunteer companies had once been filled with respectable citizens, but as these men grew older and retired, they were replaced by thugs and hoodlums. Intense rivalries developed between neighboring companies, and when an alarm was sounded the race was on to see who could reach the fire first. Unfortunately, all too often firefighting was neglected as free-for-alls broke out in the streets.

For a time the volunteers were able to use their political clout to hold off the obvious solution: replacing the volunteers with a paid fire department. The drawback to that solution was that city governments could not afford to pay the huge staffs that were necessary to man the massive hand-operated pumpers. While steam pumpers were common in England, US manufacturers had kept on making hand-operated pumpers because that was what the volunteers had demanded.

Abel Shawk and Alexander Latta of Cincinnati, Ohio provided the solution. In 1852, Shawk, a builder of hand-operated fire engines, and Latta, a railroad locomotive builder, developed a steam-powered fire engine named the 'Uncle Joe Ross' after an important Cincinnati councilman. The engine weighed 22,000 pounds (9980 kg) and required four horses, ridden artillery style, plus the propelling power of the steam engine to move it. It pumped water through a 3-inch (8 cm) hose and a 1 1/2-inch (4 cm) nozzle, with a 'throw' of 225 feet (69 m).

In those days, pumping contests between volunteer companies were frequent events, so it was only natural for the local 'vollies' to challenge that newfangled pumper, the Uncle Joe Ross. The steamer won handily. Able to do the work of six hand-pumpers, yet needing only three men to operate, the new steamer paved the way for a paid fire department in Cincinnati and other towns.

In 1859, the Cincinnati builders, confident of their steam-operated pump, challenged New York's vollies to a pumping contest. The machine faced off against the 'Man Killer,' a four-handled pumper operated by 60 of New York's strongest men. The vollies' stream of water slowly inched higher and farther than the steam pump's, but as soon as the vollies had bested the steamer, the men collapsed from exhaustion. They had won, but it was an empty victory, for the steamer was still merrily pumping water, signalling the dawn of a new era in firefighting.

By the turn of the century, horse-drawn steamers had proven to be an effective and dependable firefighting apparatus. Many steamers were capable of putting out as much water (1250 gpm/4732 l/m) as one of today's medium-sized engines. Nevertheless, the days of the horse-drawn steamers were numbered. The horseless carriage of Henry Ford, Ransom Olds and other early automakers was the wave of the future.

Automakers soon discovered that the technology required for fire apparatus differed greatly from that of the auto. Fire apparatus is generally made to order, while autos were mass produced. Moreover, powerplants on fire apparatus had to be larger, heavier and more complex in order to power both the vehicle and the pump. An interim solution was developed by John W Christie, who built Indy race cars. Christie created a front-wheel-drive gasoline powered tractor that was attached to the front of a steam engine or truck in place of horses. This innovative creation offered the best of both worlds: the economy of a gasoline motor for propulsion with the reliability of steam for pumping water.

A few automakers—Ford, Oldsmobile and Studebaker—did successfully produce some motorized fire engines, some of which can still be seen today at classic car shows. In general, however, motorized rigs were built by firms that specialized in fire apparatus. There is some disagreement as to who actually built the first motorized fire engine in the United States, but credit is generally given to American LaFrance, which delivered a motorized combination hose and chemical apparatus to the Niagara Engine Company of New London, Connecticut on 3 October 1903. Even earlier, however, around 1897, the St Louis Fire Department had a battery-operated combination wagon. Other sources cite Waterous Engine Works

Company, which developed a two-motored engine—one for propulsion, the other for pumping—for the Radnor Fire Company of Wayne, Pennsylvania in 1906. Roughly a year later, Waterous produced a single four-cylinder engine that handled both propulsion and pumping. Owned by the Fire Department of Alameda, California, this rig pumped 600 gpm (2271 l/m).

Fire chiefs all across the United States began to ponder the idea of motorized fire engines. Edward F Croker, Chief of the New York City Fire Department, bought his own Locomobile in 1901 because he couldn't wait for the city to replace the department's horse and buggy. In 1909, the Birmingham, Alabama Fire Department purchased a

Seagrave combination hose and chemical pumper. Fire-fighters were divided over whether the new motorized pumper was better than the old horse-drawn steamer so they staged a race through the center of town. The debate wasn't settled until five days later, when the two met again in a real-life race to a fire at the Birmingham-Southern College. The motorized engine whizzed past the horse-drawn steamer as it struggled up a hill, and put out the fire.

In August 1909, more than 550 fire chiefs from all over the United States met in Grand Rapids, Michigan for the annual Fire Chiefs' convention. Motorized fire apparatus was the talk of the town. Chief Hugo R Delfs of Lansing,

Right: This handsome Seagrave truck was restored in 1989 by Terry and Joel Meyers of the Twin Hills Fire Department in Sebastopol, California.

Left: This 1909 pumper was built by the Waterous Engine Works Company of St Paul, Minnesota. It is now owned by the Fairfield, California Fire Department.

Below: A 1925 Dodge Bros Chemical unit built by American LaFrance for the city of Fairfield, California. The building in the background is the San Francisco Main Library.

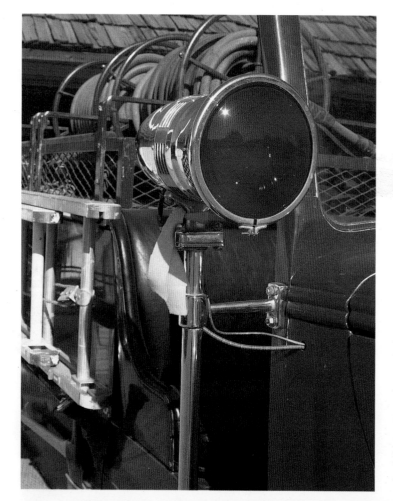

Michigan demonstrated his new 650 gpm (2460 l/m) pumper. Built by Webb on an Oldsmobile chassis, this rig cost $6500. Captain John O Glanville of St Louis reported that his motorized rigs covered three times more of the city and got to fires 50 percent faster. He added that it cost $816 a year to care for the horses, compared to $481 for the vehicles.

By 1910, manufacturers were swamped with orders for motorized apparatus. At one point, American LaFrance had orders for 10 motorized engines, sight unseen. In 1911, the Savannah, Georgia Fire Department bought seven pumpers, one chemical engine and four combination chemical and hose wagons from American LaFrance to become the nation's first completely motorized department.

In addition to American LaFrance, Seagrave, Mack, Pirsch and Aherns-Fox were among the early makers of motorized apparatus. The first three became the nation's top makers, a distinction they hold to this day. Pirsch remained in business until the late 1980s, and while Aherns-Fox didn't have the longevity of the other firms it earned a place in firefighting history with its distinctive front-mounted piston pumps and shiny silver air domes. At one point, the Chicago Fire Department had a fleet of 57, and, in testament to their durability, a 1922 model served Baltimore for 41 years.

The transition to motorized apparatus created a state of flux in the firefighting industry. Many manufacturers with only an inventory of steam pumpers were closing their doors for lack of business. Even so, not all fire

departments were ready to jump on the motorized bandwagon. Many communities had invested thousands of dollars in steamers, which still worked quite well and, in some cases, better than the new gasoline-powered pumpers. New York, for example, owned more than 300 steamers and even ordered 28 steamers as late as 1912.

Moreover, many departments were attached to the loyal horses who pulled the steamers. Though firefighters had first opposed the use of horses and had grumbled about sharing the firehouse with them, they soon fell in love with their gallant steeds. In New York, horses stayed on the job until 1922, and the steamers themselves weren't retired until 1933. Chicago's fire horses answered their final call on 5 February 1923, and Philadelphia's white stallions made their last run on New Year's Eve 1927.

Shortly after the firefighting industry became motorized, various other technological advances came along in answer to the growing number of severe fires that plagued the United States. Water towers became more powerful and ladders grew taller to match the upward climb of the nation's high rise buildings. American LaFrance built a 65-foot water tower capable of delivering 8500 gpm (32,175 l/m) for the Fire Department of New York in 1930. Pirsch built an all-powered 100-foot aluminum alloy aerial ladder for the Melrose, Massachusetts Fire Department in 1935. American LaFrance went even higher in 1941 with a 125-foot aerial for Boston.

On 28 July 1945, a B-25 bomber crashed into the 78th floor of the 102-story Empire State Building. Flames spread quickly, along corridors, through offices, down an

Above: **Though it doesn't have the distinctive Peterbilt hood, this 1939 rig is definitely a Peterbilt. In fact, it was the first fire engine built by the company.**

Right: **This 1939 Ford 95 was purchased new by Chloride, Arizona. It was shipped by rail from Detroit, Michigan to Kingman, Arizona and then driven to Chloride, a distance of approximately 22 miles. By 1991, it had only 2048 miles on the speedometer. See the photo to the *upper left* for a close-up of this beautifully cared-for engine.**

Left: **With its shiny chrome bell, this Ford from the 1920s is a work of art.**

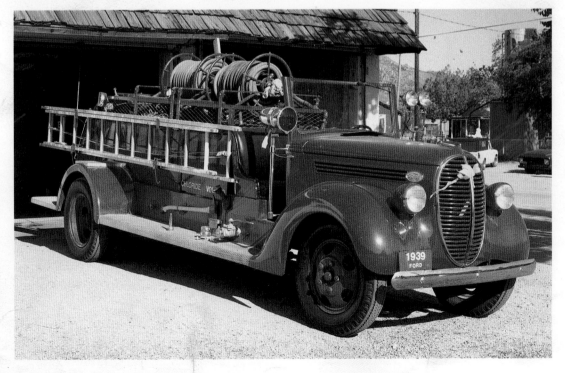

Left: A Foamite Firefoam Co extinguisher.

Above: This Hall Scott engine sits on a 1948 Mack chassis. Originally purchased by Carson City, Nevada, it is now owned by the Chloride Volun-teer Fire Department, the oldest fire department in continuous operation in the state of Arizona.

Right: A four-wheel-drive Dyna 200 pumper currently produced by Toyota.

elevator shaft and to a nearby building. Fourteen people were killed and 25 injured, but the loss of life and destruction of property could have been far greater than it was, had the accident not occurred on a Saturday afternoon when relatively few people were around. Fires are terrifying in and of themselves, but this one became a symbol of the firefighting hazards of the modern day: aircraft crashes and fires in high rises beyond the reach of the highest aerial.

A new breed of firefighting apparatus—airport rescue and firefighting vehicles—was developed to face the challenge posed by airport fires. A crash of a 747 with its 50,000 gallons (189,265 liters) of fuel can quickly turn into a monstrous inferno. In order to save the hundreds of passengers on board, the rigs used to stop these fires must be fast, large enough to carry water and/or foam to suppress the fire and be able to cross the rugged terrain that frequently surrounds an airport.

Fires in high rises are fought with snorkels and aerials, as well as special units, such as New York's American LaFrance Maxi-Water System, which are capable of delivering water at incredible volume and pressure. The New York Fire Department also has a special high rise unit equipped with a concrete core cutter for breaching floors, walls or ceilings; scaffolding for ceiling work; a portable manifold for refilling air bottles on the fire floor; and 50 oversized one-hour Scott Air Pak cylinders for breathing in smoke-filled areas. In some cases, additional support is provided by fireboats or airplanes equipped with foam.

As the firefighting industry enters the 1990s, fire apparatus makers are prepared to meet the challenge of the future, as they have since the days of the hand pumpers.

Firefighting Apparatus Today

Today's firefighting apparatus has evolved to meet the special needs of a community, whether large or small. For most cities and towns, the basic firefighting apparatus is the **pumper**, or engine, a vehicle that carries a water tank, hose, pump, ladders and portable tools. Pumpers arrive on the scene first and are positioned at the fire for best use of available water. With large fires that require more than one pumper, pumpers are designated first due, second due, and so on. Upon arriving at the scene of the fire, the driver (chauffeur in firefighter's parlance) of the first due pumper immediately hooks the rig up to a hydrant and mans the pump panel behind the cab to control water flow and pressure through one or several lines.

Pumpers are generally equipped with a centrifugal-type pump that is driven by the same motor that propels the vehicle itself. An output of 1500 gpm (5678 l/m) at a pressure of 250 psi is typical of a medium-sized pumper. Pumpers with an output of 1000 gpm (3785 l/m) usually don't have storage room for sufficient hose, so they are supported by hose-carrying trucks. Two hoses with 2 1/2 inch (6 cm) diameters will move 500 gpm (1893 l/m) of water over 1000 feet (305 m).

The booster tank on a pumper is usually 500 gallons (1893 liters), enough to extinguish small fires—a car or a trash bin. In an emergency situation, the chauffeur will start with the tank, and then head for the hydrant. But this isn't standard operating procedure, as firefighters prefer to have an infinite source of water behind them as they head inside of a building to seek out the seat of the fire.

Backing up the first due pumpers are ladder trucks with 75-, 100- or even 135-foot hydraulically powered **aerials**. The ladder is mounted on a turret that enables it to rotate 360 degrees. Outrigger jacks are used to steady the truck. Aerials are used to put large quantities of water onto a fire at a high level and for rescue work. Ladder trucks carry such things as axes, shovels, picks, ropes, pitchforks, pike poles, battering rams, bolt and wire cutters, power saws and gas and water shut-off wrenches.

The firefighter at the top of the ladder communicates via radio with the chauffeur, who operates the aerial. The rest of the crew heads inside with the picks, axes and forcible entry tools that every truck carries. The truckies' job is to ventilate the building by breaking down doors and smashing windows. The task is crucial because it allows the smoke to escape, facilitating the search for both trapped civilians and the seat of the fire. Venting also reduces the danger of backdraft—an explosion caused

when oxygen is suddenly introduced. When the fire is reasonably contained, the truckmen search the building, tearing down walls and ceilings, looking for hidden pockets of fire. Any sign of fire is immediately hit by the 'man on the nob'—the firefighter with the hose.

Ladder tenders carry much of the same support equipment as a ladder truck. Because they aren't equipped with expensive aerials, they provide many communities with a cost-effective alternative.

Elevated platforms have revolutionized firefighting. Snorkels, as they are commonly referred to, first came to national prominence in 1958 when a fire broke out at Chicago's Our Lady of Angels elementary school. Equipped with a standpipe, these platforms can throw a 1000 gpm (3785 l/m) stream through one or more turret nozzles. Because they can operate from above a fire, they provide better access to the fire and are safer than aerial

ladders, which run the risk of being hit by a collapsing wall. The basket, which can support roughly 900 pounds (408 kg), is ideal for rescue work. With their excellent capabilities, elevated platforms have proven to be superior successors to the water towers of old.

In many cases, firefighting apparatus is designed to handle particular conditions or situations. For example, cities with narrow or crowded streets once relied heavily on **tractor-drawn ladder trucks** with steerable rear axles. The firefighter steering the rear wheel is known as the tillerman. Tillered aerials are rarer these days because they have been linked with traffic accidents. American LaFrance is one of the few companies that continues to make them.

Large cities often have **rehabilitation units** where firefighters can take a break after using their allotment of compressed air in their breathing apparatus. Rehabilita-

tion units offer relief from the intense heat of a fire by providing shade and cool air via a misting system. These units also have an air conditioned area to lie down in.

Outlying areas that don't have ready access to a water supply often depend on a **tanker**, a mobile water unit equipped with a pump, hose and essential firefighting tools. The tanks on these units hold an average of 1000 to 1500 gallons (3785 to 5678 liters). A truck designed to fight brush fires would be equipped with a large water tank, and carry fire extinguishers and lots of small diameter hose.

Aircraft firefighting vehicles are equipped with foam or other fire extinguishing agents to handle the fuel fires that can break out after an aircraft crashes. The lightweight (about 8000 pounds/3630 kg) Rapid Intervention Vehicles (RIVs) are designed to arrive at the site quickly. They carry foam to last five minutes—enough time for

the backups to arrive. These big guys weigh up to 30 tons (27,000 kg) and equipped with a turret gun above the cab that shoots plumes of foam.

Rescue trucks carry a full range of emergency equipment. A partial list includes air masks, resuscitators, chain saws, rope, chair stretchers, Hurst 'Jaws of Life' tools, blankets, assorted first aid equipment and so on. The Rescue Squads of the Fire Department of New York are perhaps the best known in the world. Manned by the elite of the department, these men and women face challenges that are unheard of in most departments. New York's Rescue Squad got its start in 1915 and several from their ranks went on to become chiefs.

The handsome firefighting rigs profiled in the pages that follow represent the proud heritage of men and machine working together to protect us from one of the most destructive elements known to mankind—fire.

Left: **This Leyland DAF Water Tender is built on a chassis by Boughton. It is owned by the Lancashire County, England Fire Department.**

Right: **A Hub pumper on a GMC chassis. Hub Fire Engines and Equipment, Ltd is based in Abbotsford, BC in Canada.**

Below: **This LTI aerial serves Astoria, Oregon, the oldest American settlement west of the Rocky Mountains. The Astoria Fire Department was founded in 1870.**

FIRE ENGINES

American LaFrance

American LaFrance, the nation's premiere manufacturer of firefighting rigs, can trace its roots back to 1832, when John F Rogers began manufacturing hand-pumped fire engines known as Roger's Patent on the banks of King's Canal in Waterford, New York. Over the next two years, the company had changed hands twice and changed its name to L Button & Son.

Lysander Button and his son, Theodore, quickly earned a reputation for building quality engines. The Buttons are credited with the development of an air dome that improved the flow of water from a hand pumper. In 1862, the Button Fire Engine Company began building steam-powered fire engines, selling their first to Battle Creek, Michigan.

In 1891, the company, now called the Button Fire Engine Works, joined forces with some of the other leading manufacturers of the day to form the American Fire Engine Company. One of the nation's most prestigious manufacturers, the LaFrance Fire Engine Company, had been asked to join but had declined.

LaFrance had been formed in 1873 by Truckson LaFrance, an ironworker from Pennsylvania, who invented the rotary steam engine. Like Button Fire Engine Works, LaFrance Manufacturing Company had contributed greatly to the fledgling industry.

In 1882, LaFrance produced the first commercially successful extension ladder. The design had been developed by Daniel D Hayes of the San Francisco Fire Department in 1868. The 85-foot aerial was raised by a single horizontal worm gear turned by a long handle, manually operated by four to six men. As the gear turned, a large nut moved forward and raised the ladder. Because it was mounted on a turntable, the ladder could be swung into almost any position. Hayes' design was truly brilliant, for at that time, aerial ladders extended no more than 60 feet (18 m). The rest of the world, however, was slow to appreciate what Hayes had accomplished. He sold one rig to the

Left: **Engine No 2 of the Jacksonville, Florida Fire Department is an American LaFrance pumper.**

Right: **American LaFrance has been building aerials since 1882. This one is owned by the Astoria, Oregon Fire Department.**

San Francisco Fire Department, but its service was restricted to parades until an alarm interrupted the 1871 Fourth of July Parade and it was called into action, proving its worth. Even then, the ladder failed to receive due recognition beyond the West Coast, and Hayes sold his patent to LaFrance, which was already a leader in the fire apparatus industry. Teamed with the LaFrance name, the Hayes aerial ladder was finally recognized as a wonder of the modern world.

In 1884, LaFrance developed a piston steam engine to replace the outmoded rotary engine, and in 1894, the company built the Macomber Chemicalizer, the first pumper to combine water with salt or other firefighting chemicals. For many years, chemical pumpers helped extinguish 85 percent of all fires in their early stages.

In the late 1890s, a group of New York investors decided to create a monopoly of fire engine manufacturers and made plans to purchase all the known manufacturers from New York to St Paul, Minnesota. In its quest to control the market, the International Fire Engine Company overextended itself and reorganized in 1903 as the American LaFrance Fire Engine Company after the two major engine companies: American and LaFrance.

About 1910 fire departments around the United States, intrigued by the automobile, began to demand self-propelled fire engines. American LaFrance was the first company to produce a gas powered engine, a combination (chemical and hose) car built for Lenox, Massachusetts. Many fire departments, especially those in small communities, remained skeptical of motorized fire apparatus, doubting that a gasoline engine could power the vehicle *and* run the pumper. Horse-drawn steam engines had a proven record of dependability. Many were capable of pumping 1250 gpm (4732 l/m), which is equal to the output of today's pumpers. Indeed, the first motorized pumpers were not as good as the steamers, and until sufficiently powerful gasoline powerplants were developed, a steamer was often teamed with the two-wheel Christie gasoline tractor for motorized propulsion.

American LaFrance made its last steamer in 1914, and by this time it had successfully made the transition to motorized apparatus. From 1910 to 1926, the company produced more than 4000 pumpers, as well as aerial ladders, water towers and various other apparatus. Then, and for decades to come, American LaFrance was the number one producer of fire apparatus.

With the advent of the gasoline motor came a new hazard—oil fires. Since the late nineteenth century, 'smothering' had been recognized as a technique for extinguishing oil fires, but it wasn't until 1909 that a suitable material was discovered: a mixture of extract of licorice and bicarbonate of soda. With this discovery, a licorice importer and processor decided to enter the fire extinguishing business and formed the Foamite Firefoam Company in 1917. A decade later, in 1927, the company merged with American LaFrance to form American LaFrance and Foamite Corporation.

From the days of hand pumpers up to the present day, American LaFrance has been an innovator in the fire-fighting industry. In 1929, the company introduced its Master Series of fire apparatus, featuring such firsts as four-wheel brakes and left hand steering. The first all-steel aerial ladder with full hydraulic power appeared in 1935.

Another American LaFrance innovation was a 12-cylinder V block, 240 hp engine with a pumping capacity of 1500 gpm (5678 l/m). This revolutionary powerplant attracted the attention of other manufacturers and was soon powering Greyhound buses, the Budd streamlined electric train and armored tanks for the Army. For three decades, the V-12 powered the company's flagship fire engines.

The V-12 was a source of inspiration to Los Angles Fire Chief Ralph J Scott. As the fire chief of a major urban center, Chief Scott was forced to fight fires in heavy traffic areas. The problem was compounded by people stopping to watch the fire, adding to the congestion and making it difficult for the firefighters to reach hydrants. In 1936, a major fire broke out in a large multi-story building on Broadway in downtown Los Angeles. The traffic kept the firefighters from the hydrants near the building, and valuable time was lost as firefighters were forced to lay hose from hydrants several blocks from the fire. After this

incident, Chief Scott recognized that the solution was to hit the fire with a high-volume pumper and knock it out *before* the traffic problems made the fire department's job tougher. He proposed that American LaFrance mount two of its V-12s, one behind the other on a single chassis, doubling the output to 3000 gpm (11,356 l/m).

American LaFrance delivered the first of four Duplex pumpers to the Los Angeles Fire Department in 1938. Each pumper was capable of managing 19 hoselines or one massive water cannon. Soon after delivery, the pumpers were put to the test when a fire broke out at the Grey Building, also on Broadway in the downtown area. Three of the new engines made short work of what could have been a devastating fire.

In 1939, American LaFrance introduced a new design that would eventually become the industry standard—the cab-forward. After the war, the cab-forward was the only style offered by the company.

In 1941, American LaFrance delivered the first 125-foot (38 m) aerial to Boston, Massachusetts. A year later the truck was crushed when a wall fell on it, but the ladder itself withstood the impact and stood fully extended during the accident.

In the years immediately following World War II, the company brought out the first line of pumpers, trucks and aerials featuring a cab-forward design; a new line of dry chemical fire extinguishers; and airport crash firefighting rescue vehicles. American LaFrance remained a leader in the rescue segment of the firefighting industry, bringing out a new series of crash, rescue and airport structural fire trucks—Airport Chiefs—with special high visibility paint. The company has built more crash rescue vehicles than any other manufacturer in the United States.

In 1973, American LaFrance marked the 100th anniversary conference of the International Association of Fire Chiefs, held in Baltimore, Maryland (site of the convention in 1873), with the introduction of its Century series.

Below: American LaFrance built this custom pumper for the South Hackensack Fire Department of New Jersey. One of the oldest names in the fire apparatus industry, American LaFrance has stood for excellence for over a century.

The company is currently producing the Century 2000 series. Century 2000 pumpers have an output of 1500 gpm (5678 l/m) and are equipped with an easy-to-operate control panel featuring an Apollo 3422 monitor. The 500 gallon (1893 liter) fiberglass tank has a lifetime warranty.

To withstand the elements and harsh conditions that fire trucks are frequently subject to, the entire Century 2000 cab, body and pump enclosure are 304L low-carbon stainless steel. The rig's modular construction makes repairs quick and economical. Power is supplied by a 350-hp Detroit Diesel V-6 turbo teamed with an electrically-controlled Allison automatic transmission and Rockwell R170 axle. Cabs are available in 4-door, 7-man or 2-door, 5-man styles.

The Pacemaker series combines a wide variety of well-known cab and chassis styles with American LaFrance's all-stainless steel integral pumping modules and stainless steel bodies and aerial equipment.

American LaFrance's aerials go by the Water Chief and Ladder Chief designations. All models are available with a Century 2000 or a Pacemaker chassis and a 75- or 100-foot (23- or 30-m) aerial. The 75-foot (23-m) Water Chief is a dual purpose pumper and ladder truck. These rigs can carry up to 500 gallons (1893 liters) of water or a full 163-foot (50-m) complement of ground ladders, as well as six pike poles.

The 100-foot (30-m) model is available as a rear-mount aerial (the current trend), a mid-ship mount or the tractor-drawn variety. Once the traditional style, tractor-drawn aerials have all but disappeared from firehouses across the United States.

The Water Chief and Ladder Chief can also be equipped with the famous Snorkel water towers and articulating aerial platforms. The Snorkel basket, which holds up to 900 pounds (408 kg) and reaches 85 feet (26 m), is the ideal tool for window and roof rescues. When teamed with the Telesqurt nozzle, the tower ladder can apply a heavy water stream to windows or other hard to reach areas. The stream is controlled from the base of the tower by an electrically remote-controlled nozzle.

American LaFrance supplies fire departments across the United States with the equipment they need, whether it be a standard pumper for a small Midwestern town or the massive Maxi-Water system for the New York Fire Department. This system is composed of several interconnecting units that provide high water volume and pressure. Maxi-Water responds to greater alarm and high rise fires.

Today, American LaFrance is based in Bluefield, Virginia and is part of the fire protection, safety and security group of Figgie International, a diversified corporation. Also included in this group are 'Automatic' Sprinkler, an industry leader in fire sprinkler systems for commercial and industrial buildings; Badger-Powhatan, a fire extinguisher manufacturer; and Snorkel, makers of the famous Snorkel articulating platform that is so often seen on American LaFrance aerial trucks.

Like the Model T, a vintage American LaFrance fire engine is a highly valued collector's item. Carefully rebuilt to original specifications, these classics are displayed at antique auto shows across the country and at museums around the world. As the company motto proudly proclaims, since 1832 American LaFrance has been the standard of excellence in firefighting apparatus.

Amertek

Most people's image of a firefighting apparatus is the familiar red engine that sits at the local fire house until an alarm sends it rushing out on the street. However, firefighting sometimes requires special purpose vehicles, such as those manufactured by Amertek of Ontario, Canada. These odd-looking vehicles are specifically designed for use by the Armed Forces for firefighting at airports and military installations, both on a home base or at a tactical operations area. These vehicles are known collectively as ARFFs (Aircraft Rescue and Fire Fighting) and include the CFVR-1, the RIV-C1 and the CF4000L.

Amertek describes its CFVR-1 as a multi-role firefighting vehicle, equally capable of fighting structural fires, combatting fuel fires or suppressing outbreaks of brush fires. The CFRV-1 is equipped with a midship-mounted Godiva pump that provides up to 1000 gpm (3785 l/m) from an onboard 660 gallon (2500 liter) tank, or from draft, or from a relay pumper. What really makes this firefighting machine unusual is the roof-mounted turret gun that dispenses a gigantic plume of foam for fighting aircraft fires.

The Armed Forces favor the CFVR-1 because the design of the vehicle allows it to be driven on or off C130 and C141 aircraft without any dismantling. It can also be helicopter lifted. In addition, the CFVR-1 easily handles the unpaved roads that may be found in or around base operations, as well as the all-terrain conditions encountered at temporary tactical operations at home and abroad. Amertek has supplied the US Army with hundreds of these vehicles, many of which saw service in the Persian Gulf during Operation Desert Storm in 1991.

The RIV-C1 (Rapid Intervention Vehicle) is used by the Canadian government for airport protection across Canada. It has a roof-mounted turret gun that discharges foam at a rate of 330 gpm (1250 l/m) or dry chemicals at 15 lb/sec (6.8 kg/sec). The Godiva pump puts out 550 gpm (2280 l/m). Powered by a Detroit Diesel Allison 6V92 TA, these giants go from 0-50 mph (0-80 kph) in 20 seconds, reaching a top speed of 73 mph (118 kph). Fully loaded, they weigh 31,935 pounds (14,486 kg).

Amertek supplies its CF4000L to the US Navy. It is powered by a 400 horsepower Detroit Diesel Allison engine with a five-speed automatic transmission, accelerating from 0-50 mph (0-80 kph) in 24.5 seconds. It carries 1000 gallons (3785 liters) of water and 130 gallons (492 liters) of foam.

Though they may not look like more conventional vehicles, ARFFs are an essential element of modern firefighting.

Angloco Ltd

Angloco Limited was established in 1965 as Angloco Coachbuilders Limited. In 1972, it moved to its present location in Batley, West Yorkshire, England. Angloco's firefighting and emergency vehicles are in service in the UK, Ireland, East and West Africa, the Middle East, Indonesia, China and Hong Kong. Its customers include airports, oil refineries, municipal fire brigades, the US Department of Defense, the Civil Aviation Authority and public utilities in the UK, including the Forestry Commission, the National Coal Board, electricity undertakings and British Telecom.

The company's full range of products includes air crash rescue and rapid intervention vehicles, refinery tenders, municipal water tenders, rescue and emergency vehicles, all-terrain firefighting units, breathing apparatus appliances, control units, turntable ladders, hydraulic platforms and combined ladder platforms.

Featuring the company's own design, Angloco's Type B Water Tender carries 480 gallons (1818 liters) of water and incorporates a 2000 gpm (4540 l/m) rear-mounted gun-metal water pump. The water pump is fitted with a round-the-pump foam system, enabling foam to be produced as necessary.

Carrying a full complement of ladders and equipment including a portable pump in a side locker, the unit is suitable for combating domestic fires with two high pressure hose reels, or major fires involving hazardous materials with water from its own tank, hydrants or from open water sources.

Left: Amertek's CF4000L is used by the US Navy.

Right: The Leeds Bradford Airport uses Angloco's 8000 Air Crash Tender, a medium-sized rapid approach unit. The top-mounted turret can project a jet of foam up to 200 feet (60 meters).

Below: Strathclyde Fire Brigade, Britain's second largest municipal fire brigade, has 10 Angloco Type B Water Tenders based on the Scania G882M chassis and fitted with Scania'a factory-built four-door crew cab.

Angloco's Water Tender is based on a Volvo FL6.14 chassis and powered by a 207 BHP turbocharged and intercooled engine teamed with an Allison automatic transmission. The hydraulically tilting crew cab has room for a driver and five crew members. Included in the equipment located in the cab are brackets carrying four BA sets that can be put on by the crew while travelling to an incident and a telescopic lighting mast provides scene floodlighting.

Carrying an impressive 17,000 liters (4491 gallons) of foam, Angloco's newest foam tender—the 17000 Refinery Tender—is specifically designed for fighting major fires at refineries, industrial complexes or tank farms. Manufactured for Getty Oil of Kuwait, this immense vehicle is built on a 38 ton variant of the all-wheel-drive Mercedes-Benz 2636 chassis and is fitted with wide section sand tires for improved flotation off-road.

The PTO driven gunmetal fire pump is capable of discharging up to 2400 gpm (9090 l/m) of water when using on-site hydrants, and with its balanced foam system, can produce water and/or foam simultaneously from its six rear-mounted deliveries and roof monitor. The system's foam pump can also be utilized to transfer foam to and from the capacious full-width stainless steel foam tank.

This refinery tender is equipped with air conditioning for the three-man cab, hazardous area protection for the powerful 355 BHP engine, warning beacons, siren/public address system and searchlight with tripod and cable reel.

Angloco Air Crash Tender 8000 is a medium-sized rapid approach unit able to operate on airfield runways, service roads and soft terrain. The main pump is a midship-mounted Godiva GVA 5400 single-stage centrifugal fire pump with an output of 1321 gpm (5000 l/m). The water tank has a capacity of 1922 gallons (7274 liters), while the foam tank holds 180 gallons (682 liters) and can deliver 1009 gpm (4100 l/m) of water/foam liquid. The monitor is self-aspirating and capable of projecting a jet foam up to 197 feet (60 meters), while the vehicle is moving or stationary. A 220 lbs (100 kg) BCF unit is also provided.

Built on a Boughton Theseus 4 X 4, this tender is powered by a General Motors turbocharged diesel with an Allison five-speed gearbox. Angloco has supplied this type of unit to the Bradford Leeds Airport.

Angloco's light refinery tender is fitted with a Godiva pump with an output of 391 gpm (1590 l/m) of water and 300 gpm (1135 l/m) for two foam branchpipes with in-line inductors. The control panel is conveniently located at the rear above the pump. Storage space is provided in the rear for hose and other essential equipment. Built on a Ford Transit 190 van, the light refinery tender is powered by a Ford 2.5 liter diesel engine mated with a four-speed synchromesh gearbox with overdrive.

Angloco has supplied the UK municipal fire service with its largest firefighting vehicles—six Bronto 33-2T1 Combined Telescopic Ladder/Hydraulic Platforms in service with the London Fire Brigade. These 108 foot (33 meter) units are the highest such rescue and fire vehicles combining a telescopic rescue ladder with a 880 pounds (400 kg) capacity fire/rescue cage at the tip of an articulating boom. The cage, which can be rotated a total of 90 degrees, is fitted with a remote control monitor, stretcher support, 24 volt and 110 volt scene lighting systems.

Top left: **The Angloco 17000 Refinery Tender on a Mercedes-Benz 2636 chassis was built for Getty Oil in Kuwait.**

Left: **One of six Bronto 33-2T1 Combined Telescopic Ladder/Hydraulic Platforms supplied by Angloco for the London Fire Brigade.**

Below: **The Angloco Light Refinery Tender is built on a Ford Transit 190 van.**

Below: Built on a Volvo FL6.14 chassis, this Type B Water Tender is in service with the Dyved County Fire Brigade of South Wales.

Mounted on a 30 ton gvw Volvo Fl.10 chassis, these 8 X 4 rigs represent the state-of-the-art in chassis and aerial apparatus technology. The Volvo 318 BHP engine is coupled to an Allison five-speed automatic transmission.

Angloco recently delivered two of its Bronto Skylift Combined Telescopic Ladder/Hydraulic Platform appliances to the Bedfordshire Fire and Rescue Service and the Oxfordshire Fire Service. Both units are Bronto's 28-2T1 model.

The Bedfordshire unit is mounted on a Scania P93.Ml 6 X 4 chassis with a sleeper cab that has been modified by Angloco to carry three crew members including the driver. The hydraulic platform is fitted with a remote controlled monitor in the firefighting and rescue cage and a turret mounted portable generator supplies a 110 volt electric supply to the cage floodlamps.

Oxfordshire's unit is based on a Volvo FL.10 chassis/ sleeper cab and powered by a 318 BHP diesel engine driving through an Allison gearbox. As on the Bedfordshire unit, the platform incorporates one-sided jacking and an emergency battery drive of the hydraulic systems.

This unit also has a few special features spec'd by the Oxfordshire Fire Service: an extended outreach facility, operating at a reduced cage loading, and a deck mounted booster pump. The extended outreach facility enables the vehicle to operate over a much increased horizontal working area around the vehicle without re-siting the chassis,

thus saving critical time in rescue situations. The deck-mounted pump allows the apparatus to operate without the need for a separate water tender, provided a suitable water hydrant supply is available.

Angloco also builds a wide range of specialist support units, such a the Foam/Carrier Tender supplied to the Dyfed County Fire Service in South Wales, which covers a high risk area of oil refinery complexes and other industrial and port locations.

This Scania-based tender carries 1700 gallons (6440 liters) of foam in a compartmented stainless steel tank. Prolonged firefighting operations are possible using the deck mounted 3300 l/m foam monitor. Water is supplied to the monitor from the refinery's pressurized hydrant system, with the monitor in turn picking up foam direct from the foam tank.

The 17 ton gvw Scania G.93ML 4 X 2 chassis employs a 245 bhp engine, and a manual gearbox with computer-aided shifting. The all-aluminum alloy bodywork includes locker storage space for hose and other loose items of equipment. Audible and visual warning devices are fitted to the two man cab.

Angloco has produced an Emergency Response Vehicle—a first-of-its-kind fire apparatus—for the BASF Plc at their Seal Sands site in Cleveland. Built on a Mercedes-Benz 1120F/36 fire service chassis/cab, this Emergency Response Vehicle incorporates several features not usually found on this size of appliance. Outwardly, the unit

Left: **Angloco is the sole UK distributor for the Bronto 28-2T1 Skylift Combined Telescopic Ladder/Hydraulic Platform.**

Top right: **This Angloco Emergency Response Vehicle is now in service with BASF Plc at their Seal Sands site.**

Bottom right: **In addition to the Type B Water Tender on the** *previous pages,* **Angloco has supplied the Dyved County Fire Brigade with this Foam Carrier/Tender on a Scania G.93ML chassis.**

Left: Angloco's medium-sized Dodge 50 series-based Rescue/Emergency Tender is designed to handle a wide variety of situations.

Right: The Angloco Rapid Intervention Vehicle is built on a Volvo FL6.17 chassis. The pump handles both water and foam.

Bottom right: Angloco is the sole UK distributor for Metz turntable ladders. This model is built on a Volvo VL6.17 chassis.

appears similar to a conventional Type 'B' Water Tender, with a hydraulically tilting integral crew cab, roof mounted rescue ladders and rear locker arrangement. However, behind the rear roller shutter is a 1200 gpm (4540 l/m pump) incorporating a round-the-pump foam system, drawing water from either the on-board 480 gallon (1818 liter) tank, open water or a hydrant.

For first strike or domestic applications, two first aid hose reels are included which also incorporate a foam-making facility, with foam concentrate being carried in a 24 gallon (90 liter) stainless steel tank. For combatting incidents involving more hazardous substances, there is a 110 lb (50 kg) trolley mounted BCF extinguisher. Five breathing apparatus sets are also carried in sit-and-strap mountings behind the officer's and crew's seats.

The compact, easy-to-maneuver Mercedes-Benz chassis/cab is powered by a 204 BHP turbocharged diesel engine teamed with a six-speed synchromesh gearbox. In addition, the engine is fitted with an automatic engine shut-down valve.

Angloco produces a number of Rapid Intervention Vehicles, such as the one it built for the North Sea Gas Terminal of Total Oil Marine Plc at St Fergus. A Volvo Fl6.17 chassis/cab with 207 BHP diesel engine and manual gearbox provides the automotive power, driving both the water and foam transfer pumps via a twin power take-off system. The chassis is also fitted with an exhaust spark arrestor, engine induction shut-down valve and double pole wiring to provide on site protection.

The water pump is designed to supply the sidelines, hose reels and dual geared monitor, which has an output of 1150 gpm (4350 l/m) of foam solution. A 264 gallon (1000 liter) water tank enables the rig to move into action immediately, while connections are made to a hydrant. The pump operator then simply switches the water valve over to this supply, stopping the pump and chassis engine.

Foam production then continues, with either the monitor or sideline, drawing foam from the on-board 1321 gallon (5000 liter) foam tank. A foam transfer pump keeps the foam tank replenished from outside sources.

The RIV also features two first aid hose reels to provide first strike or domestic firefighting capabilities. In addition, the particular RIV built especially for the North Sea Gas Terminal is able to provide full operational control of the firefighting capabilities from the monitor position on the rear top deck of the unit. This enables the pump monitor to control the fire pump, vehicle engine and firefighting system so as to supply water or foam via the monitor, sidelines or hose reels, while drawing water either from the onboard tank, a hydrant supply or open water.

On the smaller end of Angloco's product line is the Dodge 50 series based rescue/emergency tender. With two lockers on each side and one full width rear-locker, this medium-sized vehicle provides ample storage for an extensive range of rescue and emergency equipment. This tender is outfitted with various electrical equipment, including two fog lamps, two blue flashing front grille mounted lamps and one hand operated officer's spotlight.

In addition to its manufacturing activities, Angloco is the sole UK distributor for Metz Feuerwehrgerate of Karlsruhe, Germany for turntable ladders. In this capacity, Angloco has supplied numerous 100 foot (30 meter) units based on a wide range of chassis such as Dennis, Renault/Dodge, MAN, Scania and Volvo to various municipal fire services.

The 100 foot (30 meter), four section telescopic ladder can be operated either from the base turret operator's position, or form the 180 kg capacity rescue cage, which can be attached to the head of the ladder. Equipment that can be used in conjunction with the cage includes a

stretcher support, water monitor, 110 volt floodlights and an intercom system. The rear bodywork has lockers for carrying equipment, hoses, jack blocks and other rescue equipment such as ropes and stretchers.

Angloco is also the sole distributor for Bronto Skylift of Tampere, Finland for combined aerial/ladder platforms; Hagglunds Vehicles of Ornskolsvik, Sweden for its all-terrain tracked vehicle, the BV 206; and Rosenbauer of Linz, Austria for fire vehicles and equipment.

Carmichael Fire Ltd

Part of the Carmichael Group, Carmichael Fire Ltd has been manufacturing firefighting vehicles since 1849. Today, it is the largest manufacturer of fire apparatus in the United Kingdom. Its product line includes everything from airfield crash and rescue tenders to foam tankers to water tankers.

Carmichael's municipal water tenders can be built on all-wheel-drive chassis from a variety of manufacturers, such as Scania or Volvo. Some tenders are equipped with aerial platforms for firefighting and rescue work. The company also builds a full line of hydraulic rescue platforms with firefighting capabilities as an option. Turntable ladders are available in varying heights and on various chassis.

Carmichael counts the UK Ministry of Defence among its customers for the First Strike foam appliance, and it supplies the UK Royal Air Force and Navy with a major airport foam Crash Tender. Carmichael's medium capacity foam vehicle with rear-wheel-drive is often used on military airfields. The company also builds a number of airport crash vehicles for use at civilian airports.

Capitalizing on its many years of experience, Carmichael also offers an extensive range of multi-purpose light fire vehicles. In fact, Carmichael prides itself on its ability to build to exact customer specifica-

Right: A lineup of Carmichael firefighting vehicles at the Welsh town of Llandundo. This is a Day Manning fire station with two water ladders, plus the turntable ladder. During the day, 'full time' firefighters remain on the premises. They man the turntable ladder and one water ladder. Retained firefighters are summoned by a beeper to crew the second water ladder. At night, *all* firefighters are at home and respond to the beeper when necessary.

Right: Based on a Mercedes-Benz 1936 4X4 chassis, this Carmichael multi-media unit carries water, foam, dry powder and carbon dioxide.

tions and offers one of the largest and most varied ranges of light vehicles in the world. A few examples of its light fire vehicles include the Redwing Light Pumping apparatus built on the Land Rover off-road 4 X 4 chassis, the Commando water and foam high-speed First Strike built on the converted 6 X 4 range Rover chassis and the All Terrain multi-media apparatus for use in remote areas such as at desert and forest fires.

As the largest manufacturer in the United Kingdom, Carmichael offers an impressive array of product support: a comprehensive stock of spare parts for all the company's products; preventive maintenance and emergency repairs; and training courses.

WS Darley & Co

In 1908, William S Darley founded WS Darley & Company in Chicago, Illinois to sell municipal supplies. While the company remains active in that area today, since 1928 it has been a respected manufacturer of fire apparatus.

At first, Darley fitted chassis supplied by their customers with pumps made by the American Steam Pump Company of Chicago, Illinois. In 1934, however, the company started building its own line of Champion pumps at a factory in Chippewa Falls, Wisconsin. Darley built its reputation on its pumps, which claim the distinction of being the only fire pumps with a lifetime warranty.

In 1949, Darley introduced the first three-stage centrifugal pump, which simultaneously provided high-pres-

Above: **This 1985 Darley Spartan model serves King County Fire District No 2 in Seattle, Washington.**

Right: **New Kingston, PA relies on this Darley pumper.**

Top right: **The Coleridge Erect Volunteer Fire Department of Ramseur, NC ordered a Darley pumper on a Ford F800 chassis.**

sure water supply from booster-hose reels plus large volumes of water from 2 1/2-inch (6 cm) and larger hoselines at conventional pressures.

As the company proclaims: 'The heart of every Darley apparatus is a Darley pump.' Darley is unique in that the company is the only apparatus manufacturer that builds both the pump and the body. Every Darley pump is engineered and assembled for the specific chassis selected, and gear ratios for each engine/pump combination are carefully selected to make the most efficient use of the engine's available power.

Today, Darley offers a complete range of apparatus and firefighting equipment: pumpers; minipumpers; tankers; drop-in units for pickup trucks; trailers complete with pump, tank, and controls; rescue vehicles; and a full range of midship, front mount and portable pumps. Its pumpers run the gamut from straight firefighting machines to deluxe units on custom chassis.

Darley's custom trucks are individually crafted to meet any specifications, while its standard Monarch or Challenger lines provide firefighting power at reduced cost. The Monarch pumper series, available in 500 to 1250 gpm (1893 to 4732 l/m) models, feature tilt-cabs for better maneuverability.

The Challenger line offers a number of custom features, including a 1000 gpm (3785 l/m) Darley two-stage pump; a pump relief valve with flush system, self-cleaning strainer, manual shutoff and dual pilot lights; a discharge check valve; totally bronze fitted pump; and a 750 gallon (2840 liter) booster tank with a 10-year warranty.

Another affordable option is the Engager series. Fitted with a Champion 1250 gpm (4732 l/m) pump, these rigs feature a fully enclosed tilt cab with seating for up to eight people.

The company moved its operations to Melrose Park, a suburb of Chicago, in the early 1960s. Still a family-owned company, Darley is run by President William Darley and Vice President Reginald Darley. A call to the company is likely to be answered by another member of the Darley family. WS Darley is a rarity in these days of international, diversified mega-corporations. It takes pride in providing a rig ideally suited to the needs of a community. Though a small company, Darley's reputation extends cross the globe, having provided firefighting apparatus for departments throughout the United States and in over 62 foreign countries.

Emergency One

In an industry in which many of the major manufacturers can trace their roots to the turn of the century, Emergency One is definitely the new kid on the block. The company was founded in 1974 by Bob Wormser, who had retired from playground equipment manufacturing and moved to Florida. Bored with early retirement, Wormser came up with a winning idea—fuel efficient fire trucks built around a prefabricated module. This concept challenged the way the fire apparatus builders had operated since the industry began.

Most manufacturers take months to complete an order, with custom jobs taking considerably longer. The prefabricated modules lowered labor costs and cut delivery time. By keeping a warehouse of truck chassis, pumps and so on on hand, Emergency One can complete an order in as little as 60 days. While budget-minded fire chiefs appreciate low costs and quick delivery time, firefighting is steeped in tradition and at first many departments were leery of a company that did things differently. Fire chiefs

Left: **Darley built this Rescue Vehicle for the town of North Greenbush.**

Below: **Delivered to the Woodbridge, New Jersey Fire Department, this Darley pumper is fitted with a 1000 gallon (3785 liter) foam tank and an 800 gallon (3028 liter) water tank.**

Top right: **Scio, New York received this Darley 1000 gpm (3785 l/m) two-stage pumper.**

Bottom right: **Built on a Ford chassis, this Darley pumper serves the Lassellville Volunteer Fire Company.**

soon overcame their prejudices, and today the company commands an impressive share of the market.

Emergency One's current lineup includes custom and commercial pumpers; quick attack pumpers; platforms, aerial ladders and telebooms; rescue vehicles; and crash fire rescue vehicles.

The Protector XL series pumpers feature aluminum water tanks with 500 to 1000 gallon (1893 to 3785 liter) capacity and single and or two-stage midship pumps, ranging from 1000 to 2000 gpm (3785 to 7570 l/m). The custom Protector XL pumper can be mounted on Emergency One's own Cyclone or Hurricane chassis. These heavy duty chassis are engineered with larger horse power engines specifically for the fire service. For optimum safety and seating, Emergency One offers a four-door, fully enclosed cab with both the Cyclone and Hurricane chassis. Up to eight firefighters can ride inside the cab—all seated and belted.

Emergency One's Hush XL pumpers are designed with a rear engine to increase cab room and decrease cab noise. A level of 78 decibels at 55 mph is substantially lower than in conventional pumpers. The quiet cab allows the vehicle to be used as a command center on the way to and during a fire. While at the scene, the quiet roomy cab can be used to cool or warm firefighters exposed to extreme weather conditions. Moving the engine also resulted in a roomier cab with seating for up to 12.

Additional safety features standard on the Hush XL include low cab steps for an easier, safer entrance and grooved aluminum handrails to let firefighters get a positive grip. Wheelbases as short as 160 inches (4064 mm) are available for maximum maneuverability.

Emergency One's line of commercial engines ranges from a 500 to a 1500 gpm (1893 to a 5678 l/m) pumper, with 500 to 1250 gallon (1893 to 4732 liter) aluminum water tanks.

Emergency One's 135 foot aerial is the tallest built in North America. The company also builds aerial ladders in heights of 75, 80, 96 and 110 feet (23, 24 and 34 m); 95 foot (29 m) platforms; and 50 foot (15 m) telebooms. All aerials have an optional pump and waterway system.

The 95 foot (29 m) platform, with a four-person capacity, is constructed entirely of high strength, non-corrosive aluminum and is equipped with an automatic, dual hydraulic leveling system and pedestal control panel.

The 50 foot teleboom can be mounted on an Emergency One or a commercial chassis. The three-section aluminum boom allows for short wheelbases, from 153 to 200 inches (3886 to 5080 cm) with no boom overhang. Tower operation is hydraulically locked in place and is functional while water is flowing.

Emergency One supplies rigs for fire departments all over the United States and Canada. A few of the company's recent customers include the Whistler Fire Depart-

ment in Whistler, British Columbia. Whistler, the number one ski resort in North America, has 220 runs on the two highest vertical drops in North America. Because of the harsh weather and difficult terrain, Whistler decided on a 95 foot platform. The all-aluminum rust-resistant aerial with a narrow jack spread allows for tight set-ups. A special hose box at the platform enables easy access to hand lines for rescues at the upper balconies of the ski lodges.

Emergency One's Protector 50 foot teleboom serves the Volunteer Fire Department of Princeton, Kentucky. The teleboom features a three-section aluminum boom that delivers 1000 gpm (3785 l/m). The ladder, cab and body are constructed of high-strength, rust-resistant aluminum.

The Fire & Rescue Department of York County, Virginia is a firm believer in Emergency One, having recently purchased six new Emergency One pumpers and one 110 foot aerial.

One of the company's new products is a dual purpose 75 foot aerial combining rescue capabilities with a 1500

gallon (5678 liter) pumper. A unit of this sort serves the Lodi, California Fire Department.

Emergency One is based in Ocala, Florida and is a subsidiary of Federal Signal Corporation. Though in operation for less than 20 years, Emergency One has already established a reputation for setting new standards in fire apparatus design.

Ford

As America's leading full-line truck company, Ford builds and sells more work trucks than any other manufacturer in the United States. Since the days of the Model T, a fair number of these trucks have seen service in fire departments across the United States.

One of the earliest models was the Fire Chief Special made for the Fire Chief of New York. A variation of the 1911 Model T Open Runabout, it was painted red

Below: This Emergency One Hurricane pumper and matching 110 foot aerial are part of the front line apparatus for the York County, Virginia Fire & Rescue Department.

Right: Fire engines built on the Ford L9000 chassis provide a dependable and economical choice for many municipalities.

and equipped with an American LaFrance bell. Model Ts were also converted into chemical and hose cars.

Throughout the 1920s, Model TT truck chassis were often paired with American LaFrance chemical and hose apparatus. Fords were also teamed with fire equipment built by such manufacturers as Oberchain-Boyer or Deluge. This trend continued during the 1930s, as small fire companies throughout the United States mounted low-priced commercial fire apparatus on a Ford 1 1/2-ton chassis. Back then a Model AA-131 chassis sold for $495, plus $25 for dual rear wheels and tires.

With the introduction of its ground-breaking V-8, Ford chassis were the choice of numerous fire departments. Following the trail blazed by its V-8 powered ancestors of the 1930s, the mid-1950s Ford F-750 became one of that era's most popular commercial fire apparatus chassis.

The F-Series and the C-Series remained favorites throughout the 1960s and 1970s, with the C-900 chassis a frequent choice of fire chiefs across the United States. Today, Ford supplies chassis for most of America's premiere makers of fire apparatus, including Darley, Emergency One, Grumman and Pierce. From the dependable F-series to the rugged L-9000, Ford remains a proven performer in the firefighting industry.

Freightliner

Freightliner, one of the leading truck builders in North America, entered the fire apparatus industry only eight years ago. Freightliner provides the chassis only, while a body builder does the body.

The company sells its FLD 120 and FLD 112 chassis for use in firefighting. The FLD 120, one of the most popular truck models in the United States, is known for its durability, while the FLD 112, with its 112 inch (284 cm) bumper-to-back-of-cab dimension, is well suited for negotiating the maze of narrow city streets.

Fulton & Wylie Ltd

When Fulton & Wylie was founded in November 1959, the company was mainly involved in building and repairing commercial vehicle coachwork, although repairing private cars also made up part of its business. In December 1968, Fulton & Wylie decided to broaden its range of activities and began constructing firefighting vehicles. The company is now the largest firefighting vehicle manufacturer in Scotland, with customers extending to many British and foreign fire brigades. Fulton & Wylie combines resources with numerous well-known chassis builders—such as Leyland DAF, Volvo and Mercedes-Benz—to offer firefighting vehicles that are safe, efficient and dependable.

The new Fulton & Wylie/Leyland DAF Water Tender is built on a specially developed version of the Leyland Freighter 16.17. The well-proven Leyland tilt cab is retained in its entirety with the exception of the rear cab wall, which is modified to give a large communication

Top left: **A winning combination—an Emergency One body on a Ford 'Cargo' chassis.**

Bottom left: **A recent entry in the fire apparatus industry, Freightliner supplied the chassis for Engine 51. The body work is by Boardman.**

Top right: **A 1990 Fulton & Wylie small firefighting vehicle based on a Ford Transit van for Highland & Islands Brigade, Scotland.**

Bottom right: **Fulton & Wylie did the complete construction from the front windshield to the rear on this 1991 Mercedes 1120-based water tender.**

opening between the driver's and the crew's cabs. The cab interior has been designed so that firefighters can don their gear and breathing apparatus while en route to the scene of the fire. The engine is the Leyland turbocharged 420, delivering 172 BHP net with either an automatic or manual gearbox. The rear bodywork is normally of all-aluminum construction in a seven roller-shutter door configuration with plenty of storage room for hoses and equipment. This tender can be fitted with a 264 or a 475 gallon (1000 or a 1800 liter) water tank, and a Godiva pump.

A similar water tender can be built on a Volvo FL6 chassis. This rig is powered by a Volvo TD61F engine paired with an Allison gearbox.

The Mercedes 1120-based Type B Fire Wizard is the latest winner from the stable of Fulton & Wylie. The monocoque construction not only affords pleasing external lines but also significantly improves the internal environment—noise levels of less than 80 decibels are the order of the day in the Fire Wizard. The rear bodywork is the well-known Fulton & Wylie standard arrangement, with pannier sides that 'tumble home' to align with the contours of the cab. This Type B water tender is fitted with a 475 gallon (1800 liter) water tank, two Collins Youldon hose reels, Akron Maurauder fog guns and a Godiva GMA 2700 pump.

Grumman Emergency Products

In 1871, the Great Chicago Fire devastated the booming city. The disaster taught the nation a brutal lesson: advanced firefighting equipment was an essential element of modern life. BJC Howe, an enterprising businessman from nearby Indiana, recognized the need and introduced a line of horse-drawn fire apparatus. Howe's family business soon established a reputation for excellence in the production of firefighting equipment.

Over the years Howe Fire Apparatus compiled an impressive list of accomplishments, including:
- the first water tank with a fully removable top,
- the first pump operator's top mount control panel,
- the first body streamlined to the cab,
- hot-dipped galvanized booster tanks with 15-year warranties as standard equipment, and
- the first production model diesel-powered fire truck.

In 1965, when Howe Fire Apparatus was approaching the century mark, it joined forces with another, smaller

Above: A Grumman Aerial-cat—America's top selling heavy duty aerial platform. At maximum extension and at any elevation, the Aerialcat delivers up to 1500 gpm (5637 l/m) with the nozzle in any position.

Right: A Grumman Wildcat pumper on a Ford F800 chassis.

Left: Fulton & Wylie Fire Warrior water tender. This is a 1979 model.

manufacturer of fire apparatus—the Oren Roanoke Corporation. Within a few years, Howe-Oren, along with Coast Apparatus, was acquired by Grumman Allied Industries to form Grumman Emergency Products.

Grumman Allied Industries is best known as the makers of the Hellcat jet fighter of World War II. Soon after the company entered the fire apparatus business, the famous 'cat' name was gracing Grumman's fire vehicles, from the Minicat to the Firecat to the Aerialcat.

At the small end of Grumman's product line is Skiddycat, one of the company's most innovative products. This small firefighter is available as a slide-on unit that mounts to a pickup truck or on a heavy-duty trailer that attaches to any vehicle.

The Minicat, as its names suggests, is a mini-pumper designed for quick initial attack, on- or off-road, or for industrial use. The strong but lightweight vehicle puts out

250 gpm (950 l/m) and carries a 250 gallon (950 liter) galvanized booster tank. Like the rest of Grumman's pumpers, the Minicat sports a pump manufactured by Waterous.

The Attackcat, a midi-pumper or rescue vehicle, is a able to maneuver through narrow alleys and bumper-to-bumper traffic. Though shorter than a standard pumper by 2 1/2 feet (.75 m), this midi has a full-size hose bed and water output of 500 to 1000 gpm (1890 to 3780 l/m). The Attackcat is available with a single or two stage Waterous pump and a 350 or 500 gallon (1330 or 1890 liter) tank.

The Firecat and the Tigercat form the backbone of the Grumman line. Both are Class A pumpers featuring a modular design on a steel subframe. The Firecat has a galvanized steel body, while the Tigercat is aluminum. Both models are available in a wide variety of chassis and drive trains, with 750 to 1500 gpm (2840 to 5680 l/m)

Waterous pumps and a 600 to 1000 gallon (2270 to 3780 liter) galvanized booster tank.

Grumman also offers a stock pumper, the Wildcat, for fire departments on a tight budget. This Class A pumper is offered in a variety of chassis, 750 or 1000 gpm (2840 or 3780 l/m) Waterous pumps, 750 or 1000 gallon (2840 or 3780 liter) booster tanks and a full-length stainless steel operator's control panel.

Grumman's tanker is called—what else—Tankercat. This economical unit, capable of supplying 1200 or 1500 gallons (4540 or 5680 liters) with a 250 gpm (950 (l/m) pump, has a modular body constructed of galvanized steel. A super pumper-tanker unit is also available. This behemoth has galvanized tanks ranging from 2000 to 3000 gallons (7570 to 11,360 liters) with pumps up to 2000 gpm (7570 l/m). The modular body is available in both galvanized steel and aluminum.

The Grumman Aerialcat is the number one selling heavy-duty aerial platform in America. The Aerialcat reaches to a working height of 95 or 102 feet (29 or 31 m) with a platform payload of 1000 pounds (453 kg) for the 95 foot (29 m) ladder and 800 pounds (362 kg) for the 102 foot (31 m) ladder.

Grumman also offers a rear-mounted steel ladder with a reach of 85 or 106 feet (26 or 32 m). A 1000 gpm (3780 l/m) waterway and air line is optional. Grumman boasts that this rig is well suited for tight maneuvering in congested city streets.

Grumman teamed up with Snorkel for a Telesqurt in 50 and 75 foot models (15 and 23 m). Snorkel articulating booms are available in working heights of 55 to 85 feet (17 to 26 m).

Grumman Emergency Products is based in Roanoke, Virginia. Though the company bears little resemblance to the small operation established by BJC Howe back in 1871, its commitment to serving the needs of fire departments across the country has never wavered. From the Minicat to the super Tankercat, Grumman has a product for every fire department.

Kenworth

Long a recognized leader among truck builders, Kenworth began manufacturing fire apparatus in 1932. In those days, the work was done by hand and building just a couple of fire engines would take six months. The second rig to roll off Kenworth's assembly line was a pumper for the volunteer fire department of Sumner, Washington. Still in service on reserve status 40 years later, it was finally retired in the late 1970s and today is called out only for parades.

Over the last 60 years, Kenworth has unveiled a number of innovative fire engines and trucks. A few of their accomplishments are highlighted below.

In 1935, Kenworth introduced a ladder truck. The sheet metal enclosing the tool compartments and ladder

Left and right: This Kenworth pumper protects San Francisco's Financial District, a densely populated area during the day. Note the low cab-forward design for easy access and improved visibility.

Below: Armed with a Kenworth pumper, the Polk County (Oregon) Fire Department battles a fire.

rack were specially made in the company's fire department shop in Spokane, Washington. That same year, Kenworth also offered a tractor with a 1908 aerial trailer that was originally drawn by horses.

A 1939 cabover, built for the Los Angeles Fire Department, was considered revolutionary in its day. This 'quad' unit provided ladder, tank, pumper and hose wagon capabilities. Another 1939 offering featured an enclosed 'canoe-style' overhead ladder rack. This unusual rig was decked out with everything Kenworth had for firefighting. The grille was made of sheet metal rather than screen, but the cab was a standard model with the doors cut off.

In 1940, Kenworth built the world's first fully automatic aerial ladder truck for the Spokane Fire Department. With the advent of World War II, Kenworth focused its energies on the war effort. By the 1950s, it was business as usual. One of Kenworth's early achievements of this decade was a 1950 ladder truck for the Seattle City Service. One of six incorporating a fully enclosed cab, this rig was modeled after a design by William Jones, Chief Engineer. Kenworth also supplied a crash truck for the Port of Seattle.

The 1951 pumper was one of the earliest designs to include a cab assembly fabricated by Kenworth, and the 1952 'Bullnose' featured a square nose adaptation of the round nose cabover designs of the late 1930s.

In 1965, Kenworth introduced a tank truck with a front-mounted, low-capacity pump. This model was in production until 1987. Though the idea for a front-mounted pump seemed innovative to many manufacturers, it was hardly new. The concept was first discussed in 1912.

In 1980, Kenworth developed a low cab-forward design for easier access and improved visibility. With the arrival of the 1990s, Kenworth continues its 60-year tradition of building innovative firefighting vehicles.

Mack

In 1900, the five Mack brothers from Brooklyn, New York successfully produced their first motor vehicle in a carriage shop. Five years later the company moved to Allentown, Pennsylvania and began producing buses, rail cars, trolleys and, of course, the trucks for which they are now known all over the world.

Mack began building fire engines in 1911 and delivered its first fire engine to the Union Fire Association of Lower Marion, Pennsylvania. Shortly afterward, Mack built its first hook-and-ladder truck. Since its early years in the business, Mack has had a close association with the New York City Fire Department and for many years had a virtual monopoly as the department's supplier. As the busiest fire department in the world, New York's preference for Mack was noted by fire departments large and small across the country.

Mack's reputation for toughness and durability applies to its fire apparatus as well as its trucks. One of the top manufacturers of fire apparatus in the United States, Mack has an impressive history. In 1915, it introduced its famous Bulldog, the snub-nosed rig that was a favorite of firefighters for generations. The company is well known for its pumpers and was the first to build a large capacity (2000 gpm/7570 l/m) triple combination pumper in 1935.

Mack topped that thirty years later with its famous Super Pumper System for the Fire Department of New York. Designed to douse a large, rapidly burning fire before it spreads, this gargantuan rig delivered an amazing 8800 gpm (33,310 l/m) at 350 pounds per square inch. The pump could also be adjusted to provide a high-pressure (700-psi) stream of 4400 gpm (16,655 l/m). By way of comparison, the Super Pumper put out four times the water at five times the pressure of a standard pumper.

The five-vehicle, 18-wheel Super Pumper System was

Previous pages: **The Whatcom County Fire District in Washington depends on its Kenworth pumper.**

Left: **The Weirton Volunteer Fire Company #1 of West Virginia is the proud owner of this distinctive Mack/Pierce pumper. This is Weirton's third Mack in recent years. The department also owns a Mack CF pumper and a Mid Liner Rescue unit.**

Right: **A pair of Mack pumpers lines up outside a West Vancouver, Canada Fire Station. The body work on these impressive pumpers is by Hub, one of Canada's best-known fire apparatus builders.**

delivered to the FDNY in October 1965 at the incredible cost of $875,000. It remained in service until the early 1980s. On the job only two months, it was called into action at a five-alarm fire at a Bronx candy factory. Roaring like Niagara Falls, water surged through the 4 1/2 inch (11 cm) hose and into Satellite 2's big cannon. Within 10 minutes, Super Pumper had the fire under control.

The Super Pumper, a 34-ton tractor and semi-trailer, was powered by a Napier-Deltic diesel engine rated at 2400 horsepower at 1800 rpm. The powerplant was connected to a six-stage DeLaval centrifugal pump made of stainless steel to allow the use of either fresh or salt water. Attached to the Super Pumper was the Super Tender, a tractor/trailer combination that carried 2000 feet (610 m) of hose specially made to handle the powerful flow of water from the pumper. Behind the Tender's cab was a gigantic water cannon that could shoot a stream 600 feet (183 meters) high. In addition, three satellite hose rigs supplied water at 2000 gpm (7570 l/m).

In addition to its famous pumpers, Mack is known for a number of industry firsts, including the first four-wheel-drive fire apparatus chassis, the first diesel engine and the first front and rear air disc brakes. In 1957, Mack took over the cab-forward design developed by Ahern-Fox, and with a few modifications turned the design into one of its major lines.

In 1964, Mack developed a fleet of tower ladders with telescoping booms for the Fire Department of New York. Able to hit fires on upper floors, Mack's Aerialscopes were designed with New York's narrow streets in mind. The telescoping design makes them easier to maneuver than a rig with an articulated boom platform.

Mack's durable powertrains are usually installed in its vehi-

cles, but customers can request engines from other makers such as Caterpillar or Detroit Diesel. If the signature Bulldog on the hood is gold, the engine is a Mack; if the bulldog is chrome, the engine was made by another manufacturer.

Mercedes-Benz

In addition to producing luxury automobiles, Mercedes-Benz produces a full line of firefighting vehicles, including crew and fire chief vehicles, tenders (pumpers), ambulance and rescue vehicles, turntable (aerial) ladders and rescue platforms, emergency tenders, tool and gear carriers and hose carriers.

The heart of the Mercedes-Benz firefighting line is its tenders, which are available in various configurations:
1. Tenders without water tanks. These vehicles pump water from open sources.
2. Tenders with water tanks. These vehicles carry water, water and foam, or a solution combining water and foam.
3. Tenders that carry only foam.
4. Dry agent tenders that carry some kind of dry extinguishing agent, such as dry powder, carbon dioxide or halon.
5. Universal fire tenders, which carry some combination of water, foam and dry agents.

Fire tenders without tanks vary in size from the 310/33 van to the U 1300 L/37. These tenders are generally equipped with a one- or two-stage centrifugal pump and, depending on the model, can transport up to 11 persons.

They are also equipped with protective clothing and gear, small fire extinguishers, hoses, valves and a variety of rescue gear, such as ladders, safety blankets, rescue lines, resuscitation equipment, telecommunication equipment, hand tools and so on.

For the fire tenders with water tanks, Mercedes-Benz uses any of its commercial vehicles fitted with a single- or multi-stage centrifugal pump. Output varies by model, ranging from 264 to 2114 gpm (1000 to 8000 l/m). Tanks carry between 264 to 2642 gallons (1000 and 10,000 liters) of water.

The Fire Team Tender LF 16 is one example from the Mercedes-Benz line of fire tenders with a water tank. Built on a Mercedes-Benz 1222 AF/36 chassis and powered by a Mercedes-Benz OM 421 six-cylinder diesel engine, this rig is equipped with a single-stage centrifugal pump that delivers 634 gpm (2400 l/m). The water tank holds 317 gallons (1200 liters) and is glass fiber reinforced plastic, unlike tanks in the US, which are generally constructed of galvanized steel. This model is also fitted with rapid intervention equipment with a 100 foot (30 meter)

stable hose. Used throughout Germany, Fire Team Tender LF 16 can carry up to nine firefighters.

The Pump Water Tender SPM/745 has a 1190 gallon (4500 liter) tank and delivers 600 gpm (2270 l/m). It is equipped with two rapid intervention sets, each with a 180 foot (55 meter) stable hose. Mercedes-Benz built this model for operation in Tanzania. It carries a crew of six.

The Large Capacity Pump Water Tender GTLF 6 sports a 1453 gallon (5500 liter) tank and 132 gallons (500 liters) of foam. The single-stage centrifugal fire pump delivers 740 gpm (2800 l/m). The remote controlled water/foam monitor puts out 634 gpm (2400 l/m) with a throw of 180 feet (55 meters) for water and 157 feet (48 meters) for foam. Additional equipment includes an automatic foam agent premixing system and two rapid interventions sets. A massive rig, the GTLF 6 is powered by a Mercedes-Benz OM 422 8-cylinder diesel engine and can accelerate from 0 to 60 km/h (37 mph) in 22 seconds.

The Airport Crash Tender FLF 11000/1350 is even larger than the GTLF 6, weighing in at 70,400 pounds (32,000 kg). The water tank holds 2906 gallons (11,000 liters), plus 357 gallons (1350 liters) of foam. The two-stage centrifugal pump is driven by a separate engine, a Mercedes-Benz OM 422, while a Mercedes-Benz OM 423 10-cylinder diesel engine powers the vehicle. Perched atop the vehicle is a water/foam monitor that puts out 1321 gpm (5000 l/m) with a throw of 246 feet (75 meters) for water and 213 feet (65 meters) for foam.

Foam tenders are generally built on two- and three-axle heavy trucks to support the large quantities of foam carried on board, generally 1057 to 2642 gallons (4000 to 10,000 liters) or more. In addition, these rigs are equipped with a centrifugal pump that draws water from hydrants or open sources; a water/foam monitor; rapid intervention equipment; and various firefighting equipment, such as protective clothing and gear, small fire extinguishers and valves. Foam tenders are manned by a driver and two crew members.

Dry agent tenders are designed to fight liquid and gas fires and are typically used at refineries, chemical works, airports and oil installations. They are built on Mercedes-Benz truck chassis with GVWs of six tons or more. These vehicles attack fires with dry powder. The tank is pressurized with nitrogen or dry compressed air to convey the dry powder. This makes the powder free-flowing and provides the necessary pressure to disperse the powder. The powder is stored in a steel container in quantities ranging from 1100 to 13,200 pounds (500 to 6000 kg). Fire tenders with a dry powder capacity of 2200 pounds (1000 kg) and more are generally equipped with a powder monitor that discharges the powder at a rate of up to 110 lbs/sec (50 kg/sec). Throw distances, assuming there is no wind, range from 148 to 246 feet (45 to 75 meters).

An example of a dry powder tender is PLF 2000, which holds 528 gallons (2000 liters) of dry powder pressurized with nitrogen from 4 X 13 gallon (50 liter) gas cylinders. The manually controlled dry powder monitor discharges 88 lbs/sec (40 kg/sec) with a throw distance of 145 feet (45 meters). Two powder guns with 100 feet (30 meters) of folding hose put out 11 lbs/sec (5 kg/sec).

Universal fire tenders employ all extinguishing agents—water, foam, dry powder, CO_2 and halon. These vehicles are equipped with single- or multi-stage centrifugal pumps delivering 264 to 2114 gpm (1000 to 8000 l/m);

a water/foam monitor; a dry powder system; a powder monitor if dry powder capacity equals 2200 pounds (1000 kg); rapid intervention equipment; and assorted fire-fighting equipment, such as hoses, valves, rescue gear and tools.

ULF 6000/1500/90 is one of a range of universal fire tenders produced by Mercedes-Benz. This rig carries 1321 gallons (5000 liters) of water, 264 gallons (1000 liters) of foam, 3300 pounds (1500 kg) of dry powder and 198 pounds (90 kg) of halon. The two-stage centrifugal pump delivers 634 gpm (2400 l/m), while the manually controlled water/foam monitor puts out 634 gpm (2400 l/m) with a throw distance of 190 feet (58 meters) for water and 174 feet (53 meters) for foam.

Mercedes-Benz turntable (aerial) ladders and Snorkels, although primarily intended for rescue operations, are nowadays increasingly being fitted with firefighting equipment. Turntable ladder DLK 44K/F, for example, is equipped with a water monitor that delivers 580 gpm (2200 l/m). The hydraulically controlled set of ladders with suspended platform can reach a height of 144 feet (44 meters). The platform can support a load of 396 pounds (180 kg). The air-conditioned cab holds six persons.

Far left, top to bottom: **A sampling from the wide range of firefighting vehicles built by Mercedes-Benz: an airport crash tender; a Snorkel; and a** large capacity pump water tender.

Below: **A pumper built by Navistar International.**

The Snorkel SS 300 is fitted with a three-arm hydraulic mast with platform. Able to rotate 360 degrees, the platform can reach heights of 100 feet (30 meters) and can support up to 803 pounds (365 kg). This model has a two-stage centrifugal pump that delivers 1190 gpm (4500 l/m) and a 238 gallon (900 liter) foam tank, while the platform itself has a manually controlled water/foam monitor.

Navistar International

Navistar International, manufacturer of the famed International trucks, promotes its 4000 Series Crew Cab as 'a truck for public service.' Designed with firefighting, construction or highway maintenance in mind, these rigs feature a heavy gauge 80 inch (203 cm) wide steel cab to withstand extreme weather conditions and rugged environments. The Crew Cab compartment is 37 inches (94 cm) longer than a standard cab, providing seating room for six firefighters. The International Crew Cab also provides a tilting fiberglass hood with integral grille and fenders for easier service and an all-bolted squared frame for straighter axle tracking to help reduce tire wear. In their firefighting role, the Series 4000 typically are spec'd as pumpers or rescue vehicles.

Oshkosh

Airport fires present a special challenge for firefighters. As thousands of gallons of fuel spew forth from a downed aircraft, the passengers and crew must be quickly evacuated from the plane before the fire turns into a raging inferno. The rigs used to bring these fires under control must be able to move quickly while transporting huge quantities of water and foam concentrate, as well as the on-board plumbing system needed to mix the foam. Add to this the ability to cross the uneven terrain that typically surrounds an airport. These requirements call for a unique vehicle—one that looks nothing like the rigs found in the local fire department.

The Oshkosh Truck Corporation of Oshkosh, Wisconsin is one of the major builders of aircraft firefighting vehicles. The company was founded in 1917 by BA Mosling and William Besserdich. Prior to World War II, the company concentrated on building all-wheel-drive vehicles for highway construction, heavy-duty hauling and snow removal. Today, the gigantic aircraft firefighting vehicles are an important segment of the company's line-up.

Vehicles range from the appropriately named Rapid Intervention Vehicle (RIV), which races to the scene for a quick assault on the fire, to the larger vehicles that finish off the job with their massive loads of foam. Oshkosh also offers a unique line of short rigs—six feet (two meters) from road to roof—that can pass under the low clearances often found in airports, such as low viaducts and hangar entrances.

Fortunately, aircraft crashes are relatively few, but if the need arises, Oshkosh rigs are ready to do the job.

These pages: **One of the leading manufacturers of airport crash and firefighting vehicles, Oshkosh supplies its vehicles to airports across the United States, as well as abroad.**

As the photo on the bottom left reveals, these enormous rigs are well-equipped to handle the rough terrain that often surrounds an airport runway.

Peterbilt

In 1939, Al Peterman, a lumber man from the Pacific Northwest, founded the Peterbilt Motors Company to build heavy duty rigs for hauling logs. However, one of the first trucks the company ever built was not a log hauler but a fire engine. This pumper was displayed at San Francisco's Golden Gate International Exposition of 1939 on Treasure Island and sold to the city of Centerville, California, later to became part of Fremont. The rig is still owned by the Fremont firefighters and is on permanent display at the Alameda County Fairgrounds. Oddly enough, the rig doesn't look much like a Peterbilt. It was built as a chassis only, with the hood as an aftermarket item.

Up through the mid-1950s, Peterbilt produced very few fire engines, almost always as special orders. Peterbilt supplied the chassis to such body builders as OH Hirst, Challenger Fire Equipment, PE Van Pelt and Coast, and

virtually all orders were shipped to destinations in California.

In the 1970s, Peterbilt began using the Model 310 for fire apparatus. That model was replaced by the 320 in 1985. The two models are similar in appearance. The low cab-forward design of the Model 320 is ideal for firefighting, as it is easy for firefighters to get in and out of while wearing 60 pounds (27 kg) of turnout gear. The horsepower is well-suited to the work, and as a regular production model it is readily available with an automatic transmission. However, some fire departments favor the Model 359, Peterbilt's flagship for many years, being produced from 1967 to 1986. Currently, Peterbilt's Model 377, a big conventional with state-of-the-art aerodynamic styling, is used for firefighting.

In recent years, Peterbilt has enjoyed a resurgence in fire apparatus, though in the grand scheme of things the numbers are very small: Out of a total annual production of 10,000 to 15,000 units, only 25 to 50 rigs end up in the fire service.

Left: There is no mistaking this handsome rig for anything but a Peterbilt. It is built on a Model 359 chassis, the company's flagship model for many years.

Above: Mill Valley, California, a wooded area with a high fire risk, counts on Peterbilt for protection.

Right: The Eagan Fire Department favors Peterbilt's Model 377, a current production model.

Overleaf: A pair of Peterbilt fire trucks on the Model 359 chassis.

Left: Engine 91, a Pierce Class A Dash pumper, serves the town of Fayal, Minnesota.

Below: In 1985, Pierce introduced the Lance series. This one was built for the Old Bridge Volunteer Fire Department of East Brunswick, NJ.

Right: Built on an IHC chassis, this Pierce Suburban unit was shipped to Adams Township in Indiana.

Pierce

In 1913, Dudley Pierce and his father Humphrey took an abandoned church in Appleton, Wisconsin and transformed it into The Auto Body Works. The company concentrated primarily on building aftermarket custom truck, taxi and bus bodies to be mounted on Ford Model T and one-ton truck chassis. By 1917, the company had added two more employees, for a total of 11, and was ready to begin construction of an office building and plant.

To protect themselves from fluctuations in orders from Ford and Chevrolet, their largest customers, company officials decided in 1927 to diversify the product line and begin building special utility bodies. To save labor, new machinery and equipment were purchased, including a body metal smoother and lacquer polishing machine. To further increase business, the company began to repair cars and trucks.

The Auto Body Works continued to expand throughout the 1930s, adding a line of utility bodies for vehicles used by power and light companies. Later, the company started supplying utility bodies for 'A' frame derricks, and from 1939 to 1941 it further expanded its line of products to include truck bodies for the bakery, brewery, furniture, beverage and refrigerated meat industries.

About this time, Eugene Pierce, the general manager, was approached about building a fire truck body on a commercial chassis. No one suspected how significant this new line would become for the company.

Over the next 15 years the company as a whole continued its pattern of steady growth. Then, in 1956, the company reached an agreement with the WS Darley Company, makers of the famous Darley pump, that enabled the fire division to expand. The following year the company began building bodies for WS Darley, a move that increased sales without the necessity of bids.

The Auto Body Works played a role in the development of the 'Snorkel' articulating boom and platform. Fitted with a basket and a hose, these units enable firefighters to attack a fire from above. It all began in 1958, when the

Auto Body Works was approached by the Pitman Company, builders of the articulating boom, to build a body for this innovative unit. After this experimental unit was exhibited at the International Fire Chiefs' Convention in Grand Rapids, Michigan, fire chiefs around the county expressed interest in the Snorkel, and by 1961 sales were increasing steadily. The booms were mounted on the chassis at the Pitman Company's plant in Kansas City and then driven to Appleton, where Pierce completed the units.

By this time, the company was known as Pierce Auto Body Works, Inc, with sales over one million dollars annually. In 1961, the company discontinued the van and beverage body line and concentrated strictly on the utility and fire business. By 1964, fire sales were up nearly 97 percent.

As Pierce entered the 1970s, it proved its ability to meet the needs of a diverse group of customers, from the US Government, which asked Pierce to build and supply spare parts for 71 P-10 rescue units for the US Air Force, to the Fire Department of Chicago, which purchased a Pierce pumper for its downtown fire station. In 1974, Pierce unveiled its first aerial platform.

With sales at 6.5 million dollars, Pierce standardized its Suburban and Mini-Pumper fire lines. In 1975, production started on an order for Saudi Arabia for 700 units, including large rescue trucks, minis, tankers and Snorkels.

In 1979, Pierce began construction of its first all-aluminum cabs. That same year Pierce obtained the rights to the Pierce Arrow name, once the maker of expensive automobiles, and used the name for its new line of alumi-

Left: **Newtown, Pennsylvania recently took delivery of a Pierce Arrow pumper.**

Below: **The Hartselle, Alabama Fire Department chose a Pierce tilt-cab D-8000 to protect their city.**

Top right: **This Pierce Lance Pumper Tanker went to the Grantville Volunteer Fire Department of East Hanover Township, Pennsylvania.**

Bottom right: **Equipped with front-wheel-drive and a rear engine, this Pierce Javelin was built for North Fort Meyers, FL.**

Top left: Tower #1 of Hamden, Connecticut is a Pierce 100 foot aerial platform.

Bottom left: The Bazetta, Ohio Fire Department opted for this Pierce 75 foot aerial ladder.

Below: Pierce builds a number of Heavy Duty Rescue vehicles, such as this one for the city of New Rochelle, NY.

num cabs. A few years later, Pierce unveiled its first built from the ground up chassis, cab and body for use on Pierce Arrow fire apparatus.

In 1984, Pierce introduced the Dash, a new cabover engine chassis with a tilt cab and four-person capacity. Still in production today, the Dash, along with its companion, the D-8000, is a Class A pumper, equipped with a midship-mounted Waterous pump and a 500 to 1000 gallon (1893 to 3785 liter) tank.

Pierce's Suburban series also continues to be a popular pumper, as does the Pierce Arrow, with its all-aluminum, four-door fully enclosed cab. The sleek Pierce Arrow features a polished stainless steel bumper and black vinyl pump panels. These rigs are offered with a choice of several Detroit Diesel engines up to 500 hp and manual or automatic transmissions.

Pierce calls its Javelin 'the ultimate high performance firefighting machine,' declaring that the Javelin 'incorporates milestone features not available from any other manufacturer.' The Javelin is equipped with front-wheel-drive; a Detroit Diesel powerplant; a midship-mounted Waterous two-stage centrifugal pump; and a 500, 750 or 1000 gallon (1893, 2840 or 3785 liter) tank. The all-aluminum cab can hold up to 11 firefighters.

Pumpers are only part of the Pierce line. The company also makes a 100 foot (30 m) aerial platform and aerial ladders in 55, 75 and 105 foot (17, 23 and 32 m) heights. The aerials can be mounted on any of their custom chassis. Pierce also offers a wide range of rescue vehicles, including a Heavy Duty Rescue series.

Today, Pierce operates three plants totalling nearly 500,000 square feet (46,450 square meters) of manufacturing space. The 'Promise of Quality' that Pierce made to its customers more than 75 years ago continues to this day with its line of fire apparatus and rescue vehicles.

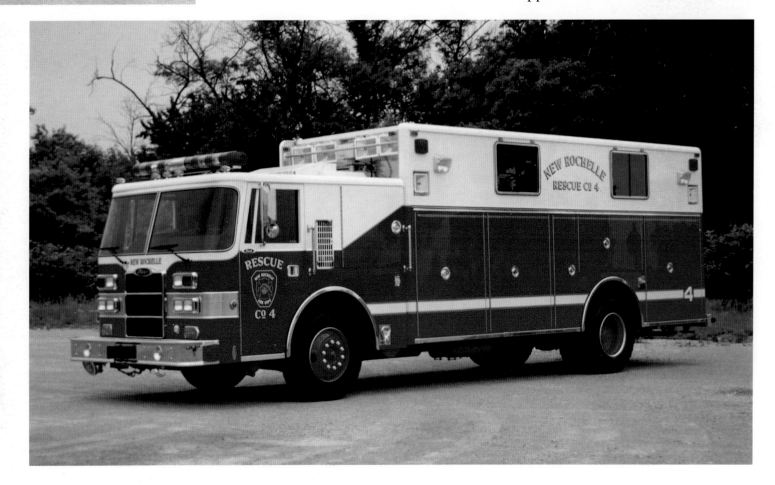

Seagrave

One of the oldest makers of fire apparatus, Seagrave has an unusual history. In 1881, Frederick S Seagrave, a Detroit businessman, started building ladders for harvesting apples from Michigan orchards.

Seagrave was a known and trusted businessman, so it was only natural that he was soon approached by the local volunteer fire department (many of whom were also apple growers) with the request that he build a rig that could be used to transport ladders to a fire. In short order, he devised a handy two-wheel rig. A shrewd businessman, Frederick Seagrave recognized a golden opportunity and turned his energy to building a hook-and-ladder truck—which proved to be an enormous success. Leaving Michigan and apples behind him, Seagrave moved his operation to Columbus, Ohio.

Inspired by the Hayes aerial ladder, which was then produced by LaFrance, Seagrave developed a mechanism to raise the ladder more quickly and efficiently. In 1901, he applied for a patent for his spring-hoist—a truly ingenious invention that revolutionized the aerial ladder industry. Other manufacturers were soon producing similar devices. Seagrave was also an early producer of water towers, which were the earliest solution for getting large volumes of water to the upper stories of tall buildings.

Word of the young company's innovative and reliable products soon spread to fire departments across the nation. In 1912, Seagrave came up with yet another brilliant idea—a centrifugal pump that discharged more water than the rotary or piston pumps currently in use. Once again, other manufacturers soon followed Seagrave's lead, and the centrifugal pump became the industry standard.

That same year saw the development of an automatic

pressure regulator, which kept pump pressure and engine speeds from fluctuating to assure a strong, steady water stream. In 1915, Seagrave added auxiliary coolers to its pumper engines to keep them from overheating, even after hours of pumping.

In 1923, Seagrave diversified its line to meet the needs of both large and small communities. Small fire departments were offered the Suburbanite, a 350 gpm (1325 l/m) pumper, while cities were wooed with the Metropolite and its 1300 gpm (4920 l/m) capacity. When American LaFrance unveiled its revolutionary V-12 powerplant, Seagrave countered with one of its own.

Over the years, the company remained at the forefront of the industry. In 1935, Seagrave introduced an alloy-steel safety ladder with a completely welded construction. It also modernized its spring-hoist aerial ladder with the development of the first fully hydraulic aerial ladder mechanism. A few years later, the company fitted all its ladders with positive locks to prevent the ladder's extensions from retracting accidentally.

Like the positive locks, many of Seagrave's innovations were designed with the safety of firefighters in mind. In 1937, for example, Seagrave developed a safety-steel canopy cab that allowed the crew to ride inside the rig rather than on the side and rear running boards where the risk of accident is high.

In addition to building safe rigs, Seagrave prides itself on building handsome ones. In 1935, Seagrave introduced a distinctive new look with a sloping grille. This style endured until 1951, when a radical new design was unveiled. That design, in turn, lasted almost 20 years.

Below: **A Seagrave 100-foot aerial ladder serves the city of San Francisco. Note the steering wheel in the back for guiding the rear axles of this big rig through city streets.**

Simon Gloster Saro

Simon Gloster Saro is the world's leading manufacturer of specialist crash fire rescue vehicles and aircraft refuellers. Firefighters in over 70 countries worldwide depend on the company's Protector line of vehicles. Cabs are double-skinned and fully insulated aluminum with a steel roll cage for safety. Chassis are available with a choice of five engines, four transmissions, two wheelbases and two width combinations.

The Protector RIV (rapid intervention vehicle) has a water capacity of 1057 to 1585 gallons (4000 to 6000 liters) and a foam capacity of 127 to 190 gallons (480 to 720 liters). Powered by a Detroit Diesel engine, the RIV accelerates from 0 to 55 mph (0 to 80 kph) in 25 seconds or less. It holds a crew of three.

The Protector C2 provides follow-up support to the RIV. Water capacity is 1585 to 1850 gallons (6000 to 7000 liters), while foam capacity is 190 to 222 gallons (720 to 840 liters). Like the RIV, the slower C2 is also powered by

Detroit Diesel engine, reaching a top speed of 80 kph (55mph) in 30 seconds.

Next in line are the Protector C3 and C4, with increased water and foam capacities. The C3 holds 2642 to 3170 gallons (10,000 to 12,000 liters) of water and 317 to 383 gallons (1200 to 1450 liters) of foam, while the C4 holds 3170 to 3700 gallons (12,000 to 14,000 liters) of water and 383 to 450 gallons (1450 to 1700 liters) of foam.

The Simon Defender line offers the cost advantage of a commercially manufactured chassis. This line can be based on any suitable 6X6 or 4X4 chassis, with or without extended crew cabs.

The Defender 6X6 has a 1850 gallon (7000 liter) water capacity and a 222 gallons (840 liter) foam capacity. The Godiva pump delivers 925 gpm (3500 l/m). The Defender 4X4 has a smaller capacity of 1190 gallons (4500 liters) and delivery rate of 793 gpm (3000 l/m).

The speedy Defender RIV can reach 80 kph (55 mph) in under 25 seconds. Fitted with a Godiva pump, the RIV puts out 634 gpm (2400 l/m). In addition to a 634-gallon (2400-liter) water capacity, it holds 143 gallon (540 liters) of foam.

The Defender Powder fights fire with a powder extinguishing agent. Its capacity ranges from 3300 to 13,200 lbs (1500 to 6000 kgs). Delivery rate ranges from 33 to 88

Left: **The Belfast City Airport of Northern Ireland relies on a Protector C3.**

Above: **A Simon Pacer Rescue unit complete with a full inventory of rescue equipment, including a self-contained rescue winch and mast lighting.**

Right: **A Defender 4 x 4 crash fire rescue vehicle protects the airport on the Isle of Man in the Irish Sea.**

lbs (15 to 40 kgs) per second, remote or manual. This vehicle has ample room for rescue equipment. The Defender line also includes a rescue vehicle, complete with elevating mast with floodlighting and a recovery winch.

The Simon Pacer line puts fast, maneuverable and efficient response in the hands of airport fore services. Designed to get to an incident across the roughest terrain in the vital first few moments, the Pacer is a superb first strike vehicle. The Pacer line is built on a GMC all-wheel-drive chassis. Cabs can be modified where necessary. The

Pacer line includes an RIV with a 317 gallon (1200 liter) water capacity and 40 gallon (150 liter) foam capacity and a Powder with a 2200 lb (1000 kg) capacity.

The Pacer Rescue has an enclosed storage area and an elevating mast. The Commander is designed for a chief officer and a crew of three. It is fitted with communications, first aid and rescue equipment. A Pacer Ambulance is also available.

Simon Gloster Saro has a long history of pioneering vehicle design, and this spirit continues with the modular design system that is at the heart of each vehicle.

Top left: **The resort area of Sun Valley-Ketchum, Idaho acquired a Sutphen aerial platform in 1988.**

Bottom left: **Sutphen delivered this 1991 custom tanker to Franklin Park, Pennsylvania in 1991.**

Below: **This 1990 Sutphen pumper is built on an International chassis.**

Sutphen

Sutphen is the largest of the small, custom fire apparatus manufacturers. Custom is the key word in describing Sutphen, for the emphasis is on manufacturing a *hand built* quality product. For over 100 years the Sutphen name has been linked with fire apparatus. CH Sutphen, the company founder, began as a salesman of fire hose. In his travels, he met many firemen and learned there was a demand for sidewalk steamers to be pulled by men, as many smaller communities could not afford stables filled with horses to pull the hose carts and wagons. In 1890, CH Sutphen delivered his first fire engine—a steam-powered pumper with a two-wheel hose reel attached—to Urbana, Ohio.

CH Sutphen's son, Harry, soon took an interest in the business and carried on until his death. In turn, his sons, Thomas and Robert, joined the business, with Robert becoming chairman of the board and Thomas, president.

The first official offices of Sutphen were in the Brunson Building in downtown Columbus, Ohio. Later the offices were moved to the Lincoln-Leveque Tower, a stately 'skyscraper' which is today a landmark in Columbus, Ohio. The very first fire truck was built in an employee's garage.

With success came the need for larger quarters, and the offices were moved to Grandview, Ohio on Dublin Road. In 1964, everything was moved to the present site at 7000 Columbus-Marysville Road in the hamlet of Amlin, now a suburb of Columbus. With many additions, the factory has evolved into what it is today.

In addition to the main plant in Amlin, which manufactures 90 to 100-foot aerials and pumpers, Sutphen operates four other plants. Hilliard, Ohio, located six miles to the south of the main plant, is the home of Sutphen

Above: **In 1987, Hartford, CT received a Sutphen 100 foot aerial platform.**

Left: **Engine 72 is a custom tanker built for the Paradise Hills Volunteer Fire Department of Bernalillo, NM.**

Top right: **This pumper for the Elma Volunteer Fire Co of Elma, NY has a stainless steel tilt cab and an enclosed pump panel.**

Bottom right: **Sutphen built this 1989 custom four-door, top mount pumper for Stuart, FL.**

Towers. Here the mini-tower, a half scale version of the 100 foot aerial tower, is constructed in a 65 or 75 foot version. The bodies of these units are manufactured in stainless steel, and customers who specify pumpers of stainless steel will have their apparatus built at this plant. Repairs, refurbs, and commercial pumpers round out the product line at Sutphen Towers.

At Springfield, Ohio, 45 miles due west of these plants, is the Sutphen Chassis Division. Neat and clean, this is the start of the Sutphen line. Name brand components are assembled into the Sutphen Custom chassis. Every item from the frame rails to the drivable chassis is handled here. Sutphen builds only one chassis line—'a deluxe custom chassis.' Drew Sutphen, Bob's son, is the plant manager and he 'speaks trucks.' A large sign near his desk proclaims 'Trucks are beautiful'; and he is constantly reviewing the chassis and upgrading to the finest new components.

Sutphen East in Monticello, New York opened its doors in June 1989 during the New York Fire Chiefs' Convention. This facility is for aerial ladder manufacture as well as repairs/service and specialty apparatus. The company's newest plant—Sutphen West—is in Kenosha, Wisconsin, and it is slated to build pumpers.

Sutphen proudly proclaims that its aerial platforms are 'unmatched in safety, performance, durability, reliability, maneuverability and appearance.' Sutphen aerials feature Hale pumps, fiberglass water tanks and 206 cubic feet (6 cubic meters) of storage compartment space. With the controls for the jack, boom and pump located in the same location, set up time takes only 15 seconds, and five people can be rescued from a four-story building in just 25 seconds. The tower can be raised, lowered, retracted, extended and so on while water is flowing. The four-section boom is shorter than a three-section and is therefore easier to maneuver.

The Sutphen 65 or 75 foot mini-tower comes with or without platforms. The deluxe cab is designed to seat six to ten persons comfortably and is available in a new four-door enclosed style. Mounted on a 200 inch (5080 mm) wheelbase, the mini-tower has a turning radius of 31 feet, 6 inches and handles like a pumper. The mini-tower is equipped with a 1000 to 2000 gpm (3785 to 7570 l/m) Hale pump, a fiberglass water tank (400 to 1000 gallon/1514 to 3785 liter) and a full complement of ground ladders. The body is heavy duty, bolted stainless steel.

The midship design turntable of the mini-tower provides a lower weight than most towers, a low center of gravity, easy access to all controls and a set up time of only 20 seconds. The aerial is fitted with an electrically-controlled nozzle, which eliminates the need for a firefighter to guide the stream, making firefighting just a little bit safer.

Sutphen builds its custom pumpers in a variety of cab styles: a traditional two-door cab with canopy, a four-door safety cab with seating for six to ten persons and a four-door tilt cab with seating for six to ten. The truck bodies are made of extruded aluminum, 12-gauge galvanneal steel or heavy duty bolted stainless steel. Like the Sutphen aerials, the pumpers are equipped with Hale pumps and fiberglass water tanks.

All of Sutphen's rigs offer a choice of Detroit Diesel, Cummins Diesel or Caterpillar engines teamed with an Allison automatic or Fuller five-speed manual transmission.

In 1990, Sutphen celebrated 100 years of operation, making it the oldest continuously operated fire apparatus manufacturer in the United States. Never owned by anyone other than a Sutphen, the company is very much a family operation, and promises to continue this grand tradition. The next generation of Sutphens is already involved in the business—it isn't at all unusual to see the Sutphen grandchildren at the plant on weekends and after school. As the company looks back at a proud 100 years of business, Sutphen is prepared to grow and change with the fire service industry.

Right: **In service at the Upper Arlington Fire Department is this 1988 Sutphen aerial platform.**

Far right, above: **A member of Engine Company No 1 of Evendale, Ohio, this Sutphen custom rescue unit is equipped to handle hazardous material.**

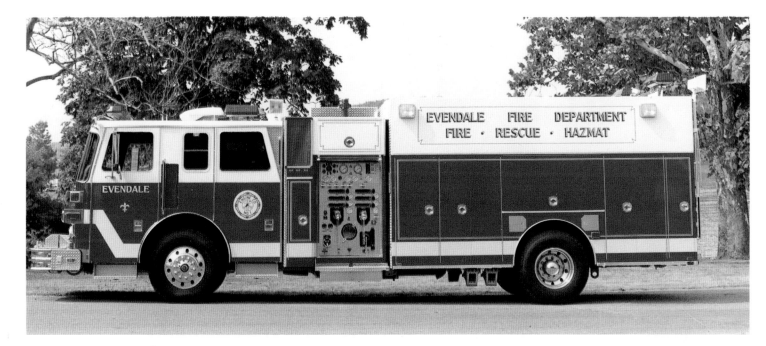

Volvo GM Heavy Truck Corporation

Like many major American truck builders, Volvo GM, makers of WhiteGMC and Volvo trucks, is involved in the fire apparatus business. In 1989, Volvo GM built two uniquely designed fire trucks for the Lebanon, Oregon Fire District. These new WhiteGMC Autocar trucks look like the sleek offspring of a long-haul tractor—except that they are equipped with four doors and three extra bucket seats. The cabs hold a total of five firefighters.

The Lebanon Fire District came up with the design in response to new National Fire Protection Association (NFPA) guidelines that call for getting all firefighters off the tailboards of their trucks while racing to the scene of a fire. (The NFPA, which is made up of fire chiefs and fire department insurance underwriters in the United States, governs firefighter safety guidelines.)

Lebanon Fire Chief Larry A Arnold explained that while hanging onto the rear of a fire truck going 55 mph and faster, firefighters sometimes fall off or 'They break limbs and they get cut. When the truck hits a bump, they can knock out their front teeth. Weather is also a factor. It's hard for firefighters to arrive on a scene and be effective if they've just had to ride in 20 degree weather.'

While most manufacturers build chassis that provide seats for firefighters, none were exactly what the Lebanon Fire District needed, as the seats faced backwards or left the firefighters exposed to the weather.

WhiteGMC, however, fit the bill. The new rigs feature a four-door cab and are powered by a Cummins 350 hp engine teamed with an Allison 750 transmission. These triple-combination pumpers are equipped with a 1500 gpm (5678 l/m) American Godiva front-mount pump, and carry water, hoses and ladders. Lebanon's new fire engines weigh in at 29,000 pounds (13,154 kg), about 4000 pounds (1814 kg) lighter than a typical fire truck.

Lebanon is very happy with its new acquisitions. The braking system is better, gas mileage has increased and, best of all, response time has improved. As Chief Arnold put it, 'We cannot think of anything on this truck to change, and that's unusual for firefighters. They are always trying to find a better way.'

Right: **Built on an Autocar chassis, this 1989 WhiteGMC fire engine was built for the Lebanon, OR Fire District. The cab was designed in response to safety guidelines established by the National Fire Protection Association.**

Far right, above: **The cab developed for the Lebanon Fire District has been used succesfully in other applications, such as this Rescue unit.**

INDEX